DEATH ANXIETY AND CLINICAL PRACTICE

Robert Langs

DEATH ANXIETY AND CLINICAL PRACTICE

Robert Langs

Foreword by

Peter L. Giovacchini

London
KARNAC BOOKS

First published in 1997 by
H. Karnac (Books) Ltd.
58 Gloucester Road
London SW7 4QY

British Library Cataloguing in Publication Data

A C.I.P. record for this book is available from the British Library

ISBN 1 85575 141 0

Edited, designed, and produced by Communication Crafts

10 9 8 7 6 5 4 3 2 1

*I wish to express my deep appreciation
to James Raney, M.D.,
who thoughtfully and with considerable wisdom
edited this book*

CONTENTS

PART TWO
Death issues and the patient

PART THREE
Death issues and the therapist

FOREWORD

Peter L. Giovacchini, M.D.

Dr Robert Langs is well known to mental health professionals. He is a prolific writer, and his contributions have been highly significant. Throughout the years he has acquired many followers who have eagerly embraced his ideas.

As usually happens with innovators, there is seldom, if ever, universal acclaim or acceptance, and Dr Langs is no exception. In some circles he is controversial and does not mingle with the mainstream. Some of his ideas, especially those dealing with the therapeutic frame, have aroused intense reactions. Since he thoroughly discusses them in this volume, I will not preempt the author.

I suppose he can be classified as a maverick in the best sense of the word (Giovacchini, 1991). In spite of the opposition he has encountered, he clings to his beliefs and continues amplifying them. There is something estimable about such dedication. He remains faithful to the analytic frame to a degree that goes beyond most classical positions. There is a purity to his viewpoint that can be both admired and questioned. As a maverick, he is not in the centre of the herd because of the extremity of his views, but he is at the periphery and still a notable member of the group.

When I was asked to write a foreword for a book on death-related conflicts and anxieties, I felt somewhat uneasy; but then I realized that my response was a confirmation of what Dr Langs was asserting. He emphasizes and decries that anything related to death is, for the most part, avoided and shunned.

There is very little in the literature pertaining to death conflicts and anxiety, especially as they are involved in the production of psychopathology and the therapeutic process. There is much resistance to confronting death-related issues in the treatment setting, both by therapists and by patients, as well as giving them the attention they deserve in a theoretical context. My initial reaction to studying Dr Langs' ideas was exactly as he predicted.

My reluctance to become involved with these topics indicates how important they are and that we cannot seek truth until we come to grips with and resolve our death anxieties. Weil (1972) puts it quite succinctly:

> Everything that is threatened by time secretes falsehood in order not to die, and in proportion to the danger it is in of dying. That is why there is not any love of truth without an unconditional acceptance of death. [p. 32]

Dr Langs unabashedly enters these forbidden and dangerous areas, his approach being both clinical and scholarly. Concerning the former, I find it difficult to accept his databases, but his discussions of the evolution of ideas concerning the concept of death and the necessity of language for its development and communication is skilful and informative. In addition to historical and cultural frames, he discusses immortality and mortality from a neurobiological perspective, much in the same way as Freud did in "Beyond the Pleasure Principle" (1920a)—but, of course, Freud's writings are updated. These sections serve as a background and foundation for Langs's theoretical concepts.

In essence, Langs returns to the topographical hypothesis, describing the architecture of the psychic apparatus as consisting of consciousness (Cs in the topographical hypothesis), the superficial unconscious (PCs or preconscious), and the deep unconscious (the Ucs). The system consciousness has limitations as to what it can integrate, and conflicted and frightening feelings about death are contained in the deep unconscious. It is interesting to see how these feelings are elaborated in the therapeutic process and how they create resistance and complications for both the therapist and the patient.

One of the signs of the awareness of the external world and individuation is the development of separation anxiety. Fear is based on the belief that the nurturing source has abandoned the infant. Perhaps at this early age the child cannot comprehend dying, but some terror of annihilation is behind the anxiety of separation and loss, and these feelings involve different levels of the psychic apparatus. There is a spectrum—a continuum—between primitive separation anxiety and the complex and subtle forms of existential anxiety. Obviously, these are basic issues and are important to emotional development and its psychopathological deviations.

Fear of abandonment, rejection, and frustration are reactions that are unavoidable during the course of emotional development. These are inherently intrapsychic responses that are in many instances reinforced by the external milieu. Finally, the recognition that life is inevitably followed by death becomes internalized and incorporated into these earlier anxieties. The latter, in turn, are counterbalanced by what might be called a life force—an impetus that seeks to explore the external world creatively—that is the outcome of being loved and nurtured.

Dr Langs refers to two types of death-related conflicts: predatory death anxiety, which can be a conscious phenomenon, and existential death anxiety, an awareness that life is transient. There is only one defence against existential death anxiety—denial, which banishes these feelings from consciousness and into the deep unconscious. There are many defensive reactions to predatory death anxiety that focus on the dangers of an abusive and assaultive environment.

In therapy, securing the treatment frame is enhancing, but it also stimulates death anxiety. The patient may feel entrapped by his commitment to therapy. The attempt to change the frame, however, leads to an acting-out of impulses that should be contained and analysed, according to the author. Health requires a successful adaptation to death-related conflicts and anxieties.

Freud used a reductionist approach as he wrote about the evolution of drives and the generative activities and immortality of unicellar organisms. The author does something like that when he discusses mental activities as having similar characteristics, and he even hints that they are derived from immune-system reactions. The mind, similar to the immune system, is more affected by trauma than by instruction. External impingements lead to the selection of defences and adaptations, and then they are stored. This process can be compared to antigen–antibodies responses.

I believe that these processes can also be understood in terms of Freud's ideas about signal anxiety in that aberrant stimuli act as triggers that lead to the re-establishment of homeostasis and defensive stabilization, much in the same way that antibodies are set into action to protect the organism. There are situations in which a person or organism deals with internal and external problems and traumas in a creatively aggressive fashion—an aggression that has been attributed to some of the T cells of the immune system. These killer cells can be compared to healthy narcissism, self-confidence, and an ample reservoir of self-esteem.

According to Dr Langs, death anxiety foments an internal level of conflict that affects many levels of psychobiological organization. Somehow, psychic structures are modified, defensively organized, and, in a manner of speaking, depleted, as happens with immune-deficiency diseases.

The author introduces some intriguing ideas concerning psychic structures. He postulates that the deep unconscious has emotional intelligence and a wisdom system. It also has a perceptual system that is involved in subliminal perception, and, according to Dr Langs, it is very sensitive to frame deviations, which, in turn, are linked to denial. Patients who want to change the conditions of the treatment setting want to be exceptions—a form of denial that death follows life. They are exceptions and not subject to this rule.

I believe that Dr Langs has presented us with cogent ideas that have to be pursued further if we are to survive as psychoanalysts. There are also moral and philosophical issues as well as clinical ones, but in all instances the question of survival is involved. There is a survival instinct that extends from a single cell to complex psychological organizations. Psychopathology often represents a maladaptive attempt to survive and maintain homeostatic stability. In these instances, clinicians are dealing with life-related conflicts.

Dr Langs is implicitly stating that such conflicts cannot be studied except as a polarity. Psychoanalytic concepts have always been cast in terms of dualism. Concerning life and death, death has received very little attention, relatively speaking. Dr Langs, in this volume, is introducing us to vistas that require further exploration and elaboration, and, in a sense, he is recapitulating the phylogeny of the development of psychology. For centuries, psychology had concentrated on phenomenology and consciousness. Freud, a dualistic thinker, stressed the other side of the conscious-and-unconscious dichotomy, by investigating the operations of the unconscious. Dr Langs, in a similar fashion, concentrates on the death part of the life-and-death duality, an uncomfortable topic but a necessary pursuit if we are to resolve our death-related anxieties and to survive as clinicians and as persons. To reconcile ourselves with death paradoxically permits us to expand our range of fulfilling life experiences.

January, 1997

PART ONE

DEATH ISSUES: BASIC PERSPECTIVES

CHAPTER ONE

A ubiquitous but elusive dread

The existential mix of human existence couples the celebration of life with the awesome awareness of the eventuality of death. Indeed, personal mortality is a compelling issue for every human being from early childhood on. Given the universality and intensity of this adaptive issue, we would rightfully expect that death-related concerns have a great bearing on emotional well-being and psychological dysfunctions—and on the psychotherapies designed to ameliorate the more disturbing consequences of death-related conflicts.

The long reach of death into human life, emotional adaptation, and the intricacies of the therapeutic process are the central concerns of this book. Given the scarcity of psychoanalytic writings in this area, the hope is to provide the reader with a deeply wrought set of much-needed perspectives and insights into the many ramifications that death anxiety has for all patients and therapists as they struggle together, in whatever fashion, to resolve a patient's emotional maladaptations in the course of a treatment experience.

AN EVOLUTIONARY PERSPECTIVE

Death and the awareness of death are products of evolutionary history. Bacteria, the first living organisms capable of metabolism and replication, are, in one sense, immortal. They flourish in their accustomed environments and do not die, but keep on dividing. They have been alive in an unbroken chain of existence for some four billion years (Margulis & Sagan, 1995).

Nature and evolution, through variation and natural selection, "elected" over very long periods to trade simplicity, asexuality, and immortality for complexity, sexuality, and mortality. Through incorporative symbiosis, one bacterium played host for another, and in time protoctists, the first multicellular organisms, evolved from these cooperative arrangements. These organisms, the first to possess nuclei, no longer simply divided by themselves but generated offspring by combining their cells with cells from similar organisms by means of an innovative sexual process. Inexplicably, this new form of replication was accompanied by the first indications of ageing and genetically programmed death—the final step in the internal metabolic histories of these new species.

As Margulis and Sagan summed it up: Death "... was the first—and is still the most serious—sexually transmitted disease" (1995, p. 41).

LEVELS OF AWARENESS OF DEATH

The *possibility* of death is an adaptive issue for all living organisms, who must, per force, possess the means of sensing and responding successfully to threats of annihilation if they and their species are to survive. This implies that the existence of death is an inevitable part of life and that inherently it calls forth a variety of defensive operations directed against the possibility of individual demise. Indeed, *the danger of death appears to be the most fundamental and universal source of adaptive and defensive structures*, and historically it has operated as a selection pressure for the development of protective activities from the beginnings of life.

The intimate connection between death and defence is sustained throughout evolution, including our own species, *Homo sapiens sapiens*. Thus, death anxiety is a significant motivating factor for all manner of emotionally relevant mental and interpersonal or behavioural defences in human beings. As we shall see, death anxiety as a critical motivating force is quite unappreciated in both psychoanalytic theory and psychotherapy practice.

The finding that 99% of all species who have inhabited this earth no longer exist—having been selected out or deleted through natural selection—attests to the great difficulty that organisms have on the deepest biological level in achieving any measure of success over the powerful threat of extermination. This adaptive problem carries over to ourselves and to the struggle that each individual inevitably wages against death, even as it becomes clear that for virtually all species—at times, including the bacteria—defeat is inevitable. The inordinate potency of the instruments of death, whether from within or outside an organism, is a remarkable and unique feature of death as an adaptation-evoking stimulus, one that affords a special cast to the defences that we and other organisms have created in order to combat and lessen its powers.

An essential feature of adaptations designed to improve chances of survival for both individuals and species is some type of *awareness* of the awesome danger of death. If we recognize that this sense of danger need not be specified definitively or articulated through language, we can define this sensibility as broadly as possible to include all types of receptor sites that evoke self-protective responses by organisms to life-threatening situations. In this light, the first vestiges of this decisive realization can be seen in the bacteria that began the evolution of biological species. Expressed in the form of an automatic chemical-based sensitivity to danger, bacteria are responsive to environmental threat—toxins and such—and they have the capacity to avoid or escape potentially fatal conditions.

In the ever-present struggle for survival, all organisms have environmentally directed sensors—sensory organs that are essential for the continuation of their lives and the opportunity to create offspring. As the nervous systems of living species increased in complexity, sensitivities to danger situations were sharpened, and the sense of threat to one's integrity became more and more palpable. Automatic and reflexive responses to peril also became increasingly complex and sophisticated.

As evolution moved forward and the neuron evolved, consciousness and awareness were developed via the introduction of *brains* and, thereby, *minds*. Organisms were able to sustain their automatic responsiveness while adding other important features to their self-protective capabilities. Mammals and other species became capable of cognitively recognizing in some non-language form the specific danger of death, primarily in the immediate moment, but with memory for situations in which their lives had been in jeopardy—places and predators that needed to be carefully avoided. By these means, they were able to create and utilize a wider range of protective and defensive measures than is possible on a reflexive basis. Chances of reaching safe quarters and of survival were greatly enhanced by these developments.

The extent and form of the awareness that a given event may prove to be annihilatory varies among animals and is most sharply realized in humans because of our ability to define and represent threats of death through *language*. The conscious representation of life-threatening dangers and of the inevitability of death as it pertains to self and others creates anxieties and adaptive issues, but these language-based depictions provide us with the most versatile repertoire of self-protective survival measures available in the animal kingdom.

These capabilities are, however, not without their cost. This cost factor arises primarily because language allows for the anticipation of the future and the definitive realization of eventual personal demise. *Death anxiety and its maladaptive consequences are the price humans pay for their extraordinary language-based survival-enhancing skills.*

* * *

Several complications related to these problems materialize as we move up the evolutionary scale. On the one hand, the evolution of neurons and neural networks—and eventually brains and minds—included the extensive development of more and more sophisticated and efficient externally directed sensory organs such as smell, touch, vision, and hearing. In addition, new internal protective mechanisms like immune systems provided a fresh array of defences against external threat, especially from microscopic predators.

But, on the other hand, along with these developments, the causes of death expanded to include not only more pervasive external threats through toxins and predators, but also through internal forms of peril resulting from dysfunctions within the organism. While many internal diseases are provoked by external events, some diseases—for example, metabolic disorders, some forms of cancer, and failures of vital organs—arise in essence from within the physical self. As a result, natural selection favoured organisms with self-healing capabilities and sensory nerve endings that were directed internally; pain endings were a central feature of this newly emerging inner-directed warning system.

In all, an arms race developed, with more and more pervasive forms of lethal danger arising from within and outside higher species such as humans on the one hand, while on the other humans became more and more efficient at detecting and combating external threat. They also proved capable of developing the practice of medicine as a means of enhancing efforts to combat the physical threat of death posed by internal and many externally caused ills. The struggles between new causes of death and new means of defeating them is an ever-present issue for all species—and for humans in particular.

PREDATORY THREAT

There were long spans of time very early in evolutionary history in which organisms thrived without the threat of predators, but as organisms evolved there came a shift from a separation of environmental niches to a sharing of space and resources that led to both cooperation and predation. The increasing complexity and fecundity of organisms and their metabolic requirements created competition for resources and also led to predatory activities—indeed, with time predators became a very real danger for virtually all living species. Predation is almost as old as multicellularity and reflects the dire necessity for organisms to supplement non-living sources of nutriment with living sources.

Predation, in the form of external or internal (via incorporated organisms) attack, is a major impetus for measures of defence. Here, too, an arms race inevitably developed between the skills of a given predator and the defensive resources of its victims—with individual and species survival the prize for the winner. The predator–prey arms race has been a major evolutionary force and selection factor throughout the history of biological species.

Predation can be conceptualized broadly to include any form of threat to a particular individual organism. In this light, we can trace an evolutionary history of predatory dangers, recognizing that threats arise largely from other species but may also come from some conspecifics (members of the same species, as seen in human cannibalism and wars). In general, these predatory threats manifestly endanger the survival of the victim in that the situation involves the blatant threat of violence and death.

The development of language and other cognitive capabilities has again placed *Homo sapiens sapiens* in a unique position vis-à-vis these issues. Humans are faced with many forms of predation that are not specifically endangering physically, nor are they concretely death-related. Nevertheless, these threats, which include non-fatal forms of physical harm and a wide range of evident and latent psychological assaults, place many human conspecifics in the role of *psychological predators*, who arouse intense forms of death anxieties and may, if pressed to an extreme, actually destroy their victims. We see again that humans possess the most elaborate resources that any species has mobilized to combat death, but they also face equally or perhaps more elaborate sources of danger.

For example, early parental deprivation or psychological assault, while not direct attempts at murder, nevertheless threaten the emotional stability of the child and usually arouse significant forms of death anxiety. The emotional maladaptations that tend to follow may be life-endangering to some degree. Other individuals may behave in ways that disturb or plague a person emotionally to the point of physical illness or self-inflicted injury. In addition there is, through language and language-related communication, an ever-present background awareness that personal death inevitably lies in the future—a psychological realization that also intensifies conflicts of humans with their predators. We see, then, that the evolved complexities of human thought, language, and emotional life both enrich our existence and complicate it greatly.

The death-related threat of self-harm highlights the mixture of external and internal factors in death anxiety in humans—environmental threats lead to inner responses that may ultimately lead to self-destructive behaviour. The latter is virtually absent in lower biological forms, which emphasizes the extent to which, in humans, self may be predator of self. A wide range of personal genetic (childhood and developmental) and psychodynamic factors play a role in these developments, and, as I shall show, so does the evolved design of the emotion-processing mind. The predatory issues faced by humans have a considerable influence on both physical and mental development and especially on the formation of both physical and mental defences. The role of death as an ever-present potential danger situation has strong and complex effects on emotional adaptation.

EXISTENTIAL DEATH ANXIETY

In addition to intensifying predatory death issues, language has created the basis for existential death anxieties—the universal human recognition and dread of eventual personal demise. By facilitating the development of the human sense of identity and self, and the capacity to anticipate the future, language enabled the well-defined articulation of the beginning and end of human life. Evidence for the connection between language use and existential death anxiety is found in the indications that the first human burial sites and religious rituals were developed about 150,000 years ago—at around the time that language first developed. No other species has the full capabilities needed to experience the anticipation of personal death, so existential death anxiety is essentially a human problem and one that has, as we shall see, enormously important ramifications.

DEATH AS AN ADAPTIVE STIMULUS

Several unique features make death per se and the threat of death powerful and difficult—and at times impossible—adaptation-evoking stimuli with which humans and other species are compelled to cope. These are, in the main, the following:

1. Death is a universal danger for all living organisms.
2. For multicellular organisms, death through metabolic failure is programmed into the genome.
3. Death caused by toxic environments or predators poses an ever-present or potential threat for all living organisms.
4. In the broadest sense of the term, the awareness of the danger or threat of death—and accompanying forms of death anxiety—is a feature of all living organisms.
5. Death appears to be the most basic driving force in the development of physical defensive measures. With the development of brains and minds, death becomes a primary source of mental and behavioural defences designed to cope with the real dangers and emotional anxieties evoked by death-related events and experiences—past, present, and future.
    a. *Mental defence* is an umbrella term that I will use to refer to the two basic emotionally responsive interrelated *mind-based* defences against death, the threat of death, death anxiety, and other forms of loss and psychological threat. Mental defences are manifest in two fundamental forms:
        i. *Communicative,* via a group of mental operations that create failures to experience and articulate via language a wide range of psychological dangers, of which death-related threats are especially prominent. This group includes a wide variety of language-based perceptual and expressive defences, the latter operating through either disguise or non-communication—as seen in the encoding or communicative obliteration of perceptions of, and reactions to, death-related experiences.
        ii. *Psychological,* which includes a broadly defined group of generally protective and adaptive efforts that are charac-

terized as psychic states and mechanisms that tend to involve the vicissitudes of the meanings of emotionally charged experiences. Prime examples are repression, a form of psychological non-recall or forgetting of definable contents, and denial, a means of obliterating observable reality.

b. *Behavioural defence* entails all manner of actual activities that are, consciously and unconsciously, in the service of emotional defensiveness. In general, this type of action response is carried out without thought of the issues to which it is an unconscious response.

6. Individual incidents of survival-threatening danger may be met with successful adaptive responses in that it is possible to master death-related predatory dangers. However, humans, through language and direct observation of death or its portrayal, develop at an early age a persistent awareness that ultimately there is no way to triumph over death as one may triumph over an adversary, environmental threat, or harmful relationship—that is, sooner or later all humans must fail in their efforts to master the existential danger of death. The inevitability of adaptive failure regarding personal death is a striking and fateful feature of human experience, and, as I shall show in some detail, this fact greatly affects the nature of the mental and behavioural defences against death-related events that humans have evolved.
7. In organisms with advanced body configurations incorporating brains and minds, the danger of death may arise from outside or within an organism, including from the minds of others and of oneself.
8. As a danger situation and stimulus for adaptive response, the possibility and inevitability of death always involves both physical and truly life-threatening dangers, and psychological or emotional ones. Most of the other sources of emotional threat, such as interpersonal conflicts, the loss of a loved one, a home, or a job, also involve a combination of both actual harm and emotional upset. Thus, intrapsychic conflicts, which are essentially confined to the psychological realm, nevertheless typically have real, external evocative triggers. Often these non-

death experiences are linked unconsciously to death and evoke conscious and especially unconscious forms of death anxiety. Death appears, then, to highlight the mixed nature—both real and imagined/emotional—of human danger situations.

9. In addition to life-threatening situations, humans have a unique source of death anxiety in their language-based ability to anticipate definitively the future demise of self and others. There are, then, two basic forms in which the awareness of death and death anxiety are articulated, each with its own configuration and consequences:

   a. *Death as a physical danger.* The awareness *of predatory and toxic threats of death,* internal and external, involves death as a danger situation that calls forth capacities to recognize and actively cope with life-endangering events. *Here, then, the awareness of death and death anxiety primarily serve to mobilize and sharpen adaptive responses and resources so as to enhance chances of survival.*

   b. *Death as an existential fact.* The existential awareness of death and *existential death anxiety* involve the ongoing recognition of the inevitability of death for oneself and other humans and living creatures. *Here, the awareness of death and death anxiety have largely disruptive effects. Existential death anxiety does, however, have mixed effects that may mobilize adaptive resources or, alternatively, may overwhelm these resources and cause adaptive failures and dysfunctions.*

10. Each form of death awareness and death anxiety is a factor in defence formation, although the kinds of defences they promote tend to differ.

   a. *Predatory–danger forms of death anxiety* prompt the development and use of physical and mental coping mechanisms designed to enhance an individual's perception and awareness of danger, and to shore up adaptive resources capable of repelling the threat of annihilation. In this type of danger situation, there is hope for survival, and, as a result, active survival strategies, physical and mental, short- and long-term, are honed and favoured.

   b. *Existential death anxiety,* on the other hand, is unaccompanied by realistic hope for survival and tends therefore to promote the development and use of awareness-obliterating, denial-based defences designed to reduce rather than sharpen one's awareness of the threat of death. Within limits, these obliterating, non-communicating, blind action, denial types of mental defences are in the service of overall adaptation. However, the overuse of these defences—a common occurrence—is quite maladaptive and has many detrimental consequences.

11. The spectre of death takes a variety of forms, of which some *are manifest and self-evident*, while others are *disguised* and recognizable only through a full appreciation of their unconscious meanings.

    a. There are, then, death-related experiences like serious illness and injury, which tend to be *manifestly* realized. But there are also *latent* death-related experiences whose links to death and death anxiety are entirely unconscious. For example, every event involving a ground rule or frame, whether the frame is secured or modified, has an unconscious death-pertinent meaning (see chapter 13).

    b. The clinical investigation, interpretation, and management of the unconscious meanings of *manifest* death-related events and of *latent*, unconsciously experienced death-related impingements, are essential features of effective psychotherapy.

12. Just as death issues have both conscious and unconscious representations, so *defences* against death anxiety operate both consciously and unconsciously as well.

    a. *Conscious-system defences* involve direct and known efforts to cope with death-related issues.

        i. For *predatory–danger of death* situations, these defences are a vital part of an organism's efforts to survive an immediate threat of eradication. They tend primarily to be physical—such as forms of fight or flight, activated reflexes and chemical/hormonal responses, tachycardia, medical interventions, etc.—although mental defences also play a role. Indeed, conscious-system defences are our prime resource against the immediate threat of being destroyed by an environmental or inner threat.

ii. For *existential death anxiety*, the defences tend to be more mental than physical because little can be done actively to combat the awareness of the inevitability of personal demise. These mental defences include both forms—communicative and psychological. While there are indeed some ways in which we consciously defend ourselves mentally against existential death anxiety—such as by trying to avoid the subject or by directly denying an illness that is a serious threat to personal survival—most of the defences directed against this form of concern about death operate quite unconsciously, because, except in the case of acute existential crises, the presence and manifestations of existential death anxiety are, as a rule, not consciously recognized as such.

b. *Deep-unconscious-system defences* are also shaped by and responsive to death issues.

i. With respect to *predatory–danger of death situations*, unconscious defences and other resources such as unconscious perceptiveness and understanding are of little adaptive value because they have little or no effect on conscious or direct coping efforts (Langs, 1995, 1996). Information and meaning that are perceived and processed unconsciously have no direct access to the conscious mind and are therefore not especially relevant to or useful in death-associated emergency situations where prompt and effective response is critical to survival. At times of crisis, the deep unconscious system shuts down, and the mind operates almost entirely with its conscious-system resources (see chapters 6 and 7).

ii. With *existential death anxiety*, deep unconscious defences appear to be the main means used to fend off and adaptively reduce these ever-present concerns. These protective measures operate psychologically, communicatively, and behaviourally. Indeed, there is a powerful link between how and what we experience psychologically, what and how we communicate, and how we behave on the one hand, and death issues on the other. Many missing elements in communicating, aspects of forgetting, and manic/celebration forms of action are unconsciously designed to deny or otherwise defend against existential death anxiety. These defences can be detected, however, only when the specific adaptation-evoking, death-related triggering events for a given set of responses are known.

* * *

To summarize: death is a danger situation that operates as a selection and causative factor both in long-term evolutionary change and in the development of individual defensive resources and the resultant capabilities for immediate adaptation. Understanding in depth the dangers posed by death, the potential of death concerns as a stimulus for creativity and growth, and the burdens death places on human lives and minds is vital if we wish to appreciate the vicissitudes of emotional life and the process of psychotherapy. In the chapters that follow, the many ramifications of these propositions are further developed.

CHAPTER TWO

Death themes, manifest and latent

While affects, intuition, empathy, and action play a role in psychotherapy, the essence of the treatment experience is conveyed through words. Meaning, experience, interaction, communication, and adaptation are most tellingly language-based. Indeed, the other aspects of the therapeutic experience cannot be precisely formulated or understood without addressing the words and contexts that characterize their nature and meanings. Grasping the problems posed by death itself and by the threat of death and death anxiety similarly requires language-based formulations, whatever affects it may arouse.

LANGUAGE AND DEATH

The development of the great adaptive resource of language for both internal representation and communication is perhaps the most distinctive feature of our species, *Homo sapiens sapiens*

(Bickerton, 1990, 1995; Langs, 1996; Lieberman, 1991). Language allows for a well-articulated sense of personal identity, a capacity for reflective self-awareness, the ability to remember definitively and to think about the past and anticipate the future, and an incisive sense of me versus not-me, self and not-self or other.

Language also enables humans to develop a clear sense of death as the inevitable outcome and conclusion of life. While predatory danger of death is often a matter of non-language physical threat, the existential promise of death tends to be articulated chiefly through language. However, the verbal and non-verbal aspects of a death-related experience tend to intermingle in that every brush with the threat of physical death arouses psychological death anxieties. These experiences activate the existential form of the fear of annihilation as well—the real danger of death is a distinct reminder of its inevitability.

On the defensive side, the obliteration of language-based representations is, as noted, a major means of coping with the existential form of death anxiety. In addition, the predatory danger of death mobilizes emergency protective actions, with thought and language playing a vital, but often secondary role. However, the development of long-term protection against predatory and toxic forms of death tends to make ample use of language in the forms of reasoning, planning, strategizing, and establishing guides for action.

DIRECT RECALL

Personal death per se is a major life issue, but death anxiety is also aroused by many other kinds of death-related and non-death experiences. While mammals like the apes show depressive and other limited responses to the death of other members of their species, none of this is articulated via language or established as lasting internal representations. Only humans have an awareness of a vast variety of death-connected incidents and possibilities that, once identified or experienced, are retained in language-defined memory, consciously and unconsciously, for much of a lifetime.

Sooner or later, and in most cases rather early in life, every individual experiences the loss through death of a family member, friend, or other person of some importance to him or her. In addition, the threat of death may arise because of an illness or injury in others, and, quite importantly, in oneself as well. Many types of separation and non-death loss experiences also contribute to this constellation of death-related events, and separations and endings of all kinds are forever linked both to the predatory–traumatic and existential forms of death and to the related death anxieties. Language and the emergent well-defined sense of self that it facilitates in humans enable *Homo sapiens sapiens* uniquely to link these loss-related experiences to themselves as they continually attempt to cope with their personal death as the end of self. The many facets of death as the end of life are most vividly and explicitly represented in human consciousness.

A given person's *separation, illness, injury, and death profile or life history,* which includes all death-related events and the individual's responses to them, has a profound effect on his or her emotional life and, of course, on any engagement he or she has with psychotherapy. This history with all of its ramifications is stored unconsciously in *two forms* within two very different systems of *the emotion-processing mind,* which is the cognitive mental module with which we adapt to emotionally charged stimuli or triggering events (Langs, 1995, 1996).

The first memory system is set within *the conscious system* and is *called the superficial unconscious subsystem of the conscious system.* The representations within this system have minimal or no disguise and are *directly accessible to awareness.* They are, however, subjected to a conscious-system repressive defence (barriers to direct recall) that serves as a filter for awareness.

The death-related memories in this system tend to be (1) manifestly about death, injury, and illness, and (2) to be retrievable in manifest, unencoded form. These memories are stored and minimally processed within the superficial unconscious subsystem and are then recoverable mainly through the process of *direct recall.* This recollection process must often overcome conscious-system repressive defences so that, at times, effort must be made to undo the forgetting involved—much of it, again, in the form of striving to remember aspects of a death-related event in some undisguised fashion.

> For example, Ms Gentry is in therapy with Dr Gordon, a male psychologist. Midway through a session in the first year of her treatment for depression, Dr Gordon announces that in two months, he will be taking a week off. After acknowledging the announcement, the patient recalls and recounts aspects of the death of her mother. She then speaks of a friend of her mother's who is ill and has become addicted to sleeping medication. This story evokes the recall of a forgotten aspect of her mother's death, namely, that her mother had become addicted to a pain medication which had contributed to her demise.

In this brief vignette,[1] the therapist's announcement of a vacation triggered the recall of the death of the patient's mother. And while these images encode aspects of the patient's unconscious experience of her therapist's impending absence, for present purposes I shall focus on their manifest meanings. In that regard, we can see that the patient was manifestly recalling and working over the loss of her mother. In doing so, she omitted and repressed a relatively painful aspect of this death experience—the mother's addiction to painkillers. But all it took for the patient herself to modify this *conscious-system repressive barrier* was to create a thinly disguised representation of the repressed contents (her mother's ill and addicted friend), which then immediately brought forth the missing part of the memory.

The mental defences here took the forms of *conscious-system psychological repression and communicative obliteration or non-communication* regarding the mother's use of drugs. And, as is typical of conscious-system defences, the patient herself was able spontaneously to modify the barrier and allow the repressed memory segment direct access to conscious awareness.

---

[1]The vignettes offered in this book are entirely fictitious. They do, however, faithfully reflect clinical experience and are offered to illustrate and provide a narrative sense of the main points to be developed in the book.

ENCODED RECALL

The second type of unconscious memory storage of aspects and meanings of death-related events takes place *in the deep unconscious system of the emotion-processing mind.* This deep unconscious storage-memory subsystem relies on *unconscious perception* for its acquisitions. Once registered unconsciously, these deeply repressed impressions and meanings are processed, but the results of this processing and the memories themselves have *no means of direct, undisguised access to awareness.*

The contents that are under deep-unconscious-system repression are different from those that are under conscious-system repression, and the repressive barriers themselves are different as well. Where the contents under conscious-system repression have originally been registered consciously and are directly retrievable, most of the contents under deep-unconscious-system repression have originally been registered *unconsciously* and can be retrieved only in *encoded form*—there is no direct recall of these contents whatsoever.

These deeply repressed contents tend to be of three kinds:

1. Extremely threatening aspects of death-connected events that do not register consciously, but are subliminally perceived and processed in the deep unconscious system.
2. An extremely traumatic death-related event that is consciously perceived and then shunted to the deep unconscious system, where it is kept under repression in a form that is no longer available to direct recall.
3. The death-related meanings of all non-death-related events that are unconsciously connected with death and evoke death anxiety. The death-connected meanings of these events are unconsciously perceived and stored in the deep unconscious system's memory storage subsystem, from which, as indicated, they cannot find direct but only encoded expression. *The most common class of these disguised and unconsciously experienced death-connected incidents pertains to ground rule and frame-related events and their management.*

These contents are under *deep-unconscious-system repression*, in that the repressed experience and its meanings cannot in any way access direct recall. In order to have a conscious experience of these contents, the deeply repressed segment and meanings must be activated by an immediate triggering experience within the psychotherapy—these are virtually the only events that activate the workings of the deep unconscious system and stimulate its encoded communications. *Trigger-decoding* this disguised material (i.e. deciphering its encoded meanings in light of its immediate adaptation-evoking triggering event) will, then, under optimal conditions, allow for the repressed memory to find decoded, conscious representation and access to awareness. In this way, the emotion-processing mind's natural use of disguise is undone and deep insight achieved.

It is not possible to decode these encoded representations of deep-unconscious-system-repressed memories in isolation, because they do not find expression in the absence of an activating triggering event. The deep unconscious system of the emotion-processing mind is an adaptive system that generates encoded narrative imagery only when it is responding to an immediate stimulus, usually in the form of a ground-rule-related intervention—the class of triggers to which the system is most sensitive.

It is, then, only when a current frame-related triggering intervention activates the representation of a deeply repressed death-related event and its deeply repressed meanings that this type of deep repression can be modified and the missing meanings find encoded representation. Thus, while superficially repressed contents emerge from repression whole cloth, deeply repressed contents emerge from repression only in encoded, disguised form.

The deep unconscious system therefore has two types of repressive capacities:

1. Maintaining a forgotten event or meaning unconsciously without encoded representation.
2. Maintaining an event or meaning in a state that allows it to be expressed in encoded form through narrative communications: It is only through the trigger-decoding of the *encoded or deriva-*

tive representations of a deeply repressed event or meaning that access to consciousness is finally achieved. In addition, trigger-decoding modifies conscious-system repression in that quite often a trigger-decoded interpretation is followed by the direct recall of superficially repressed memories that are connected to the interpretative material.

A clinical illustration

In a session several months after the one from which the earlier clinical example was taken, Dr Gordon unexpectedly announced that he would be out of his office at the time of Ms Gentry's session the following week.

After acknowledging the cancellation and stating that it was all right with her, she had a lot of errands to run in any case, Ms Gentry told a story about a man who was accused of murdering a female jogger. The story reminded her of a movie she had seen in which a husband tried to kill his wife.

Dr Gordon trigger-decoded and interpreted these narrative themes as *his patient's unconscious experience of his sudden cancellation of her session as an act of murder.* Ms Gentry responded by mentioning that the murderous husband in the film was a genius inventor who had patented several new machines, but who also invented a number of murderous devices. This idea of a man trying to kill his wife brought her father to mind. He was a tinkerer of sorts. The idea of murdering a wife was somehow connected in her mind to a vague sense that Ms Gentry had, but had never put into words, that her father had pushed the pain medication at her mother—that in some sense he had killed her.

Here, then, the patient's unconscious perception of her father's contribution to the death of her mother had registered unconsciously rather than consciously and had then been processed in the patient's deep unconscious system as an act of murder. The patient's associations did not facilitate the direct recall of this deeply repressed impression, which had achieved derivative representation only in response to the triggering event of the therapist's sudden cancellation of the patient's session. The trigger had activated the memory in part because it recalled a deeply repressed aspect of a past event and in part because it served to convey an unconscious perception of the therapist's frame-related announcement.

It took the trigger-decoding of the immediate unconscious meaning of this disguised derivative to enable the patient to link the same encoded story to the trigger of the death of her mother. It was only then that she was able to modify the deep repressive barrier that was obliterating her impression of her father's role in the death of her mother and allow that impression finally to enter awareness.

UNCONSCIOUS REGISTRATION

There are, in principle, three circumstances under which aspects of a death-related experience enter the deep unconscious rather than the conscious system and thereby become inaccessible for direct recall. These conditions are similar to those delineated above to account for deeply repressed contents, but they bear elaboration:

1. The death-related experience may be of such traumatic intensity and shock that even though it registers consciously and initially is stored in the superficial unconscious subsystem, its shock value renders it irretrievable directly, and it becomes a part of the deep-unconscious-system memory (storage) subsystem. Once it is so located, it cannot be accessed directly but requires activation by an immediate frame-related trigger within the therapy and trigger-decoding to be reconstructed or recalled directly.

   Examples of this kind of traumatic triggering event are acts of extreme violence, like murder, which subsequently may be entirely repressed by the perpetrator or an observer, or the latent, death-equivalent experience of a child who is molested by a parent.

2. The second cause for unconscious perception and registration of a death-related experience arises through meanings and implications that are, from the outset, so anxiety-provoking that they are perceived unconsciously rather than consciously. These meanings are automatically barred from direct access to awareness by an unconscious screening device, a *message analysing centre*, and directed towards unconscious perception. They are then processed outside awareness by the *deep unconscious wisdom subsystem* (the processing system of the deep unconscious system) and stored in the deep unconscious memory subsystem. They are retrievable only in a manner similar to the first type of deep unconscious memory—that is, solely through the trigger-decoding of encoded representations.

   Examples of this kind of triggering event or death-related meaning include especially anxiety-provoking aspects of death-related traumas (as seen in the previous vignette), the perception of a non-obvious illness in a loved one that is not consciously registered, or a trauma like a minor car accident, which seems of little consequence on the surface but evokes unconscious perceptions of the experience that connects it to and arouses severe death anxieties.

3. Finally, unconscious perception is selected when a death-related experience is manifestly unrelated to events materially connected with death, such as illness, injury, and other forms of harm and loss. With this type of trigger, the connection to death anxiety is not manifestly evident and therefore does not register consciously. The activation of death anxiety becomes apparent only when the narratives that are evoked in response to the trigger in question are trigger-decoded.

   For example, a therapist's securing or modifying a ground rule is consciously experienced as managing the framework of the therapy. But unconsciously, *all frame-related interventions by therapists have a connection with issues of death and dying*. Frame modifications—such as cancelling a session, or changing the time of a single session, or a self-revelation by a therapist—are unconsciously experienced as assaultive and murderous of the patient: they consistently evoke *predatory forms of death anxiety*.

On the other hand, therapists' frame-securing interventions are experienced unconsciously as sound and enhancing, but also as confining and annihilatory. They consistently evoke *existential forms of death anxiety* related to the inevitability of death—an anxiety that has its own, distinctive persecutory qualities. This arises because securing a frame is enhancing for the patient and yet entrapping as well—it establishes a rigid commitment to the therapy.

Another vignette

To cite a relevant clinical example that involves an *anticipated trigger*, Mr Wile was in therapy with Ms Mills because he was unhappy about being unable to relate well to women. About a year into treatment, he began his session by asking whether Ms Mills would reduce her fee from $90 to $75. He had had to send his mother $5,000 to pay off some money she had borrowed and as a result he was in financial trouble himself.

Ms Mills responded [correctly] by simply asking her patient to continue to say whatever came to mind. Mr Wile paused, and then his thoughts wandered to a situation at work, where his salary had been cut. This was a nasty piece of business—the boss had been dishonest and exploitative in not sticking to their agreement. It was no way to treat an employee.

Ms Mills trigger-decoded this disguised imagery by pointing out that Mr Wile had asked for a reduction in his fee and had gone on to speak of a salary cut that violated an agreement and was a dishonest and exploitative act that should not have happened. It seemed clear that the story addressed his proposal that she reduce her fee and take a salary cut herself, and that it indicated that to do so would violate their contract and allow him to exploit her in a dishonest manner. His encoded recommendation to not do it made sense in this light, and she would take his advice and hold the fee where it is.

Mr Wile thought for a moment and then smiled and said he was thinking of the quote from Hamlet—neither a borrower

> nor lender be. The fee reduction would be like having the therapist lend him money or, better still, be a way of making her the one who lent his mother the $5,000. His brother, who is wealthy and does well with finances, had advised him not to lend his mother the money—adding that she would probably spend it on candy and clothes, as was her habit.
>
> The clothing brought an odd story to mind. He had seen on television a drama about a man who would dress up in women's clothing and then take men to his apartment, tie them to a chair, and assault them physically. He killed two of his victims before he was apprehended. At times life seems so purposeless and unpredictable—only death is certain.

This vignette illustrates the deep unconscious processing of an *anticipated* frame-altering trigger—a reduction by the therapist of the patient's fee. The patient's encoded, derivative message was properly trigger-decoded by Ms Mills and her intervention obtained *encoded validation* through the quote from Shakespeare and the story of the well-functioning, financially wise brother. But the derivatives then changed their tone, and the patient conveyed a powerful image of entrapment and murder, followed by an allusion to the emptiness of life and the certainty of death. These are best seen as encoded expressions of the persecutory existential death anxieties that were activated when Ms Mills kept the frame of this therapy unchanged and secured. Much as the gift of life comes at the price of death, so the gift of a secured frame comes with the price of activated existential death anxieties—issues that tend, however, to be more readily worked through towards a measure of resolution in a secured-frame context than they are in a modified frame.

Secured frames, after obtaining encoded validation for their health-giving aspects, consistently arouse existential death anxieties but render them available for working over and fresh adaptive solutions.

> In a session later in the therapy, Mr Wile asked Ms Mills to change the time of his next session because he had an appointment with his internist. Ms Mills had wanted to be free at the

> time of the patient's appointment, so she rather quickly [erroneously] complied with her patient's request.
>
> Turning to free-associating, Mr Wile went on to tell another story about his brother, but this one was about how his brother was always trying to manipulate the patient and trying to get him to do things he should not do.
>
> Recently, Mr Wile had been supposed to have dinner with their father, but the brother talked him into meeting him and a mutual business associate first, so he was late in meeting his father. His father was furious with him for not being on time for their appointment, and Mr Wile was furious at his brother for getting him to do something that he knew would mess up his commitment to his father. Once he had arranged to see his father that night, he should not have done anything that would jeopardize meeting him as planned. When he finally met him, his father was so upset that he began to hyperventilate and complained that his sons were trying to murder him.

Typically, when the frame or ground rules of a therapy are altered, the patient's encoded narratives will speak against the frame change and reflect unconscious perceptions of the frame change as destructive and persecutory—an attempt at murder, as in the story encoded here.

Frame-related interventions, whether frame-securing or frame-modifying, are the most common class of non-manifest, death-anxiety-evoking stimuli with which humans are compelled to deal.

EVOCATORS OF DEATH ANXIETY

We have seen, then, that there are two classes of adaptation-evoking triggering events that arouse death anxiety and activate the conflicts and issues related to death to which virtually every human must, over time, adapt. Some of these occurrences are danger-of-death situations, others are more closely tied to existential death anxieties. To summarize, the following classes of triggering events are certain to evoke active forms of death anxiety and efforts to adapt to these anxieties:

1. *Self-evident death and death-related events.* The first class of death-related events includes a variety of happenings that are linked to death via loss, separation, harm, and endings. They include:
    a. *Death*—of loved ones and others, including animals.
    b. *Illness and injury*—of self and others, including animals.
    c. *Physical deprivations and the loss of protection and nutrients.*
    d. *Destruction*—of inanimate objects like houses and office buildings; of places like forests; of cities and countries; etc.
    e. *Loss*—of body parts like fingers and limbs; of objects and possessions like jewellery and cars; of people like spouses, children, colleagues, and friends; of living quarters; of jobs or schools; of money and other resources; etc.
    f. *Change of space or quarters*—physical moves such as translocating to another city or changing offices.
    g. *Interruptions,* like vacations or breaks in relationships.

    In these instances the link between the triggering event and death anxiety is clear in that the event either brings up the possibility of death or involves an experience that touches on the evident meanings of death, such as loss and interruption.
2. *Events that are linked to death not consciously but unconsciously and are expressed without a clear allusion to a manifest death-related theme.*
    a. *Forms of emotional deprivation and harm*—as seen with emotional abandonment and in sending contradictory messages that are unconsciously intended to drive another person crazy and to suicide.
    b. *Unconsciously communicated death wishes and desires to harm or hurt someone*—as reflected in a wide range of encoded stories about violence and harm that imply wishes to harm the listener.
    c. *All frame-related behaviours and interventions*—as seen in psychotherapy when, as noted above, both frame-securing and

frame-modifying actions by either patient or therapist evokes one or the other type of death anxiety.

* * *

With this in mind, we turn now to some further aspects of the relationship between death-related issues and the psychotherapy experience.

CHAPTER THREE

Death anxiety and psychotherapy

As I have indicated, death is a universal and inherently unresolvable adaptive issue, and conscious and unconscious forms of death anxiety are ever-present. As a result, these grave concerns are significant factors in the development of virtually every type of emotional dysfunction.

But here, too, there is a notable trade-off. Whereas on the one hand maladaptive and failed attempts to adapt to death-related issues and the anxieties they arouse contribute significantly to emotional disturbance, on the other hand efforts to cope consciously and especially unconsciously with death anxiety are a source of considerable inventiveness and creativity. Thus, the successful negotiation of death anxieties may contribute to emotional health or emotional ills, depending on how they are negotiated. In addition, *emotional health requires that an individual successfully adapt to his or her death-related conflicts and anxieties.*

The widespread effects of death and death anxiety similarly infiltrate virtually every aspect of the psychotherapy situation. Death-related issues consistently play a major role in the therapeutic process. However, many of these effects, which are quite strong, go unrecognized because the influence operates indirectly and outside direct awareness—unconsciously. Both parties to therapy are under rather unrelenting pressure to adapt within the treatment situation to the plethora of death-connected adaptation-evoking stimuli that arise in their personal lives and especially in their shared therapy experience.

INDICATIONS OF ACTIVATED DEATH ANXIETIES

We have begun to explore the ways in which death issues arise in psychotherapy and psychoanalysis, terms I use interchangeably. Indications of the activation of death-related conflicts take both direct and indirect (implied) forms. The former involve manifest allusions to death and related subjects, while the latter involve communications and behaviours that typically are evoked or triggered by death anxiety.

The underlying death issue and anxieties may involve predatory or existential types of danger of death, although mixtures of both types are commonplace. In general, existential death anxiety is ever-present and will reveal itself in various ways in response to a variety of triggering events. However, the inevitability of personal death is always aroused by predatory death-related experiences, though the reverse is seldom the case—primary activators of existential death anxiety generally do not involve situations of psychological harm or physical threat.

Death issues should be considered whenever any of the following materialize from the patient:

1. *Direct signs of activated death anxiety:*
    a. Allusion to death in any context whatsoever—a communicative indicator.
    b. References to the death-related themes, conscious and unconscious, referred to in chapter 2—a communicative (thematically expressive) indicator.
    c. The patient has been referred to the therapist because a

previous therapist has become disabled or has died—a communicative (thematically expressive) and behavioural indicator.

2. *Indirect signs of activated death anxiety:*

   a. The patient enters therapy after a prior therapist has terminated the patient's therapy prematurely—a communicative (thematically expressive) and behavioural indicator.

   b. The patient makes an effort to modify the ground rules of the therapy or requests that the therapist do so—a communicatively defensive and behavioural indicator. As will be shown, all efforts to modify the framework of therapy are based on notable issues with death and the anxieties it evokes (see chapter 13). These actions also serve to obliterate direct and especially indirect or encoded allusions to death-related events and issues.

   c. The patient intellectualizes for long periods of time and fails to bring forth narrative images—a defensive communicative indicator based on unconscious efforts to prevent the emergence of direct and encoded allusions to death-related issues.

   d. The patient prematurely introduces the termination of his or her therapy, including real threats to leave treatment—a defensive behavioural indicator. Activated death anxieties are the most common underlying cause of flights from a treatment experience.

   e. The patient engages in harmful actions (so-called acting out) or in evidently maladaptive or pathological behaviours—a behavioural/symptomatic indicator.

   f. The patient shows new symptoms or exacerbations of existing or previously resolved symptoms—a behavioural/symptomatic indicator. Maladaptations, symptomatic regressions, and interpersonal disturbances almost always have some at least partial basis in activated, unresolved death anxieties.

   g. The patient is injured or falls ill—a behavioural/symptomatic indicator that involves a death-related event. This particular sign of active death anxiety may take either an indirect (non-life-threatening) or direct (life-threatening) form.

The comprehensiveness of this list indicates that death is by no means an intermittent problem (and therapeutic opportunity) in psychotherapy, but an unremitting one. This pervasiveness becomes clear when we recognize the more subtle signs of its presence. Clinically, for example, a study of sessions drawn from an intensive type of communicative psychotherapy called *empowered psychotherapy* (Langs, 1993), which maximizes a patient's narrative communications, has revealed that virtually every session contained notable death-related themes and clear indications of death-related conflicts. All in all, there is considerable evidence that in psychotherapy the exploration and resolution of death-related concerns and anxieties play an indispensable role in a therapist's efforts to enhance the patient's adaptive resources and resolve his or her emotional dysfunctions.

LIMITATIONS OF MANIFEST APPROACHES TO DEATH ISSUES

The ubiquity of death-related expressions and conflicts in psychotherapy calls for an expanded approach to these problems by psychotherapists. Effective therapeutic work requires a full understanding of manifest and latent, conscious and unconscious, manifestations of death anxieties. To use this as a basis for extending our therapeutic efforts in death-related issues, we need to appreciate two aspects of the situation: (1) the limitations of manifest content approaches to this area, and (2) the basis on which the unconscious meanings and maladaptations that pertain to death issues can be explored, meaningfully interpreted, and curatively modified.

There is a growing literature on the subject of death and psychotherapy, much of it rooted in Freud's writings on the death instinct (Freud, 1920a) and Becker's (1973) well-known book, *Denial of Death*. The psychoanalytic literature is highly theoretical and touches on questions related to the psychobiological need to die, the relationship between this need or instinct and aggression, and similar concerns. The psychotherapy writings are more practically oriented and are focused on the elderly and on dying and seriously ill patients, most often involving malignancies and the AIDS-related syndromes—patients for whom death is a realistic threat.

All of these approaches are based on formulations of manifest contents and their implications, without an appreciation for encoded meaning and the adaptation-evoking events that activate these meanings (see chapter 5). This focus on surface issues and evident psychodynamics misses the powerful and complex unconscious forms of death-related conflicts and communications and the deeply unconscious issues raised by life-threatening and lesser types of illness. In addition, non-death, latent (disguised) death-related problems, especially those that stem from the interventions of therapists, are missed entirely.

Therapeutic work based on manifest listening and formulating is, then, limited in two basic ways:

1. It is confined to consciously known, manifest death concerns and does not deal with latent or unconsciously evoked and expressed death-related issues such as those aroused by frame-related interventions.
2. It is conducted entirely on the manifest level of communication, supplemented at times with the exploration of easily decoded unconscious elements drawn from the superficial unconscious subsystem of the conscious system. Such manifest concerns are far less powerful in their effects than those experienced on the deep unconscious level.

These restrictions lead to the avoidance of many of the highly disturbing conflicts and experiences created by these existential and predatory death-related crises. Both patient and therapist are thereby spared painful imagery and meanings, but these aspects of the situation remain unrealized and uninterpreted—they continue to wreak havoc for the patient's emotional life. Avoidance is a costly defence in regard to death anxiety, even when it is unwittingly and unknowingly utilized.

Illness in the patient or a death-related experience in connection with a patient's loved ones or a close associate constitute external death-related triggering events—that is, they do not directly involve or emanate from an intervention by the therapist. Clinical study indicates that with very few exceptions, patients work over their external death-related experiences manifestly, with little use of encoded narrative, considerable intellectualizing, and the offer of undisguised connections between the current trauma and past traumatic experiences. In essence, then, the reactions of patients in psychotherapy to external death-related events tend to be confined to conscious-system responses with little or no deep unconscious processing.

Therapists who address these issues directly limit themselves to conscious-system-adaptive efforts without addressing deep unconscious responses of far greater power. They miss the critical ways in which the patient's allusions to an external trigger event, and his or her associations to the event, *encode deep unconscious perceptions and adaptive responses to a very different and significant adaptation-evoking trigger constituted as an intervention, usually frame-related, by the therapist.* Displacement operates continuously in human adaptation and is critical to the means by which unconscious experience is revealed in psychotherapy. Manifest content approaches to death issues cannot effect deep inner change in patients because they entail a failure to realize that allusions to external traumas virtually always have two levels of meaning: manifestly, they pertain to the trauma itself, and latently, they allude through disguise to some recent intervention of the therapist.

WORKING WITH DEEP UNCONSCIOUS RESPONSES TO DEATH ISSUES

The deep unconscious system's responses to death-related triggers can be addressed and worked with in ways that lead to improvements in adaptation that conscious-system efforts cannot achieve. The general failure of therapists to recognize and address their patients' extremely important deep unconscious responses to death-related traumas/triggers is not merely a cognitive failure. It reflects the pervasive defences that are aroused by these issues in both patients and therapists (see below). To appreciate the issues involved, I offer an outline of how therapeutic work with death-related issues can be expanded to include the operations of the deep unconscious system.

The key to this enlargement lies with an understanding of the architecture of the *emotion-processing mind*—the two-system, cognitive mental module that is responsible for emotional adaptations, conscious and unconscious (Langs, 1995, 1996; see chapter 6). To focus here on the deep unconscious system of the emotion-processing mind, the critical features of this system as they apply to the clinical exploration of death issues are the following:

1. The deep unconscious system has a perceptual apparatus that operates via unconscious or subliminal perception.
2. The system focuses on the here-and-now situation and relationship. In therapy this is the immediate therapeutic interaction and the interventions of the therapist.
3. The system restricts itself almost entirely to ground-rule- and frame-related interventions (with secondary concerns for the extent to which the therapist is pursuing deep unconscious meaning and is intervening validly). This means that in therapy patients' deep unconscious systems are continuously processing the adaptation-evoking triggering events that involve therapists' frame-interpretative and -management efforts. This concentration is inborn and a psychobiological feature of the human mind.
   a. Therapeutic work with deep unconscious experience is therefore feasible only through the exploration, interpretation, and frame-management responses that stem from the patient's encoded material, which emanates from this system.
4. In psychotherapy, then, exploration of the deep unconscious responses to death-related triggering events takes place meaningfully only through addressing the patient's encoded and

behavioural responses to death-related triggering events that arise from the therapist's interventions and behaviours. Two types of interventions or occasions are most often responsible for the arousal of death anxieties:

a. An illness or injury of the therapist that is self-evident to the patient, mentioned by the therapist (a major technical error), or revealed by a third party. All such revelations, whether inadvertent or unavoidable, are experienced by the patient as frame-modifying departures from the ideal, secured frame of therapy which assures the patient of the therapist's relative anonymity (Langs, 1992). They are responded to accordingly by the deep unconscious system.

    i. In regard to the death of a therapist, the situation is complex because the working-over must take place with another therapist (see chapters 14 and 16). As a result, most of the patient's encoded deep unconscious responses will be focused on the present therapist, and much of the reaction to the death of the former therapist will be conveyed manifestly and reflect conscious-system reactions to the loss. Some minimal encoding may occur under these circumstances, but the patient's use of manifest allusions to the prior therapist must be understood by the current therapist as a means of also encoding the patient's unconscious experience of the immediate therapist's recent interventions and the framework of the present treatment situation.

b. All frame-related interventions by therapists arouse death anxieties in their patients. Frame modifications evoke predatory anxieties, while frame-securing efforts evoke existential forms (see chapter 12).

5. These insights should alert therapists to the kinds of interventions and events within therapy that activate their patients' death anxieties and lead to the appearance of pertinent encoded derivatives. Trigger-decoded interventions (efforts that link the encoded themes in the patient's narrative material to their activating triggers) will reveal the patient's unconscious experience of a death-related triggering event within therapy and

define the patient's unconsciously expressed, frame-related, and other healing correctives as well.

6. To reiterate, this understanding indicates that allusions and associations to external triggers must be treated both manifestly in terms of conscious responses and latently as encoded messages. In therapies in which frame-related interventions, especially those that are frame-modifying, are abundant and unconsciously traumatic, these outside hurtful events serve admirably to disguise and encode the patient's experience of the therapist's work. It requires considerable mastery of a therapist's own death anxieties to forego undue defensiveness and to stay focused on the deep unconscious death-related meanings of patients' material.

KEY FACTORS IN ADAPTING TO DEATH ANXIETY

At least six basic factors affect how patients (and therapists) adapt to death-related issues. Knowledge of the sources of patients' resistances and pervasive defensiveness in this area should help therapists to understand, tolerate, and appreciate how these obstacles (and their own defensiveness) are best resolved. The key areas of influences on adaptation to activated death anxieties are:

1. *The evolved design of the emotion-processing mind.* The basic architecture of the human mind is the foundation for human efforts to adapt to death-related issues. The evolved design features of this mental module were selected under environmental conditions that involved many death-related issues. As a result of these selection pressures, which eventually included realizations of the inevitability of personal demise, the architecture of the emotion-processing mind favours obliterating defensiveness over active coping efforts and automatically relegates many aspects of death-related experiences to unconscious perception and processing (Langs, 1995; see chapter 6). These unconscious responses are retrievable solely through trigger-decoding.

2. *Psychodynamic and personal genetic factors.* An individual's coincident life history of manifest and latent death-related traumas, conscious and especially unconscious intrapsychic and interpersonal conflicts, and issues of self-regulation and self-maintenance play a significant role in the way that person copes with immediate death-related triggering events.

3. *The impossibility of full mastery of death anxiety.* Death-related triggering events evoke existential death anxieties that afford dealing with death an aura of helplessness and hopelessness. This unforgiving aspect of death shapes adaptive responses and pushes them again more towards denial than trying actively to cope.

4. *The after-effects of death-related traumas.* Almost without exception, death-connected traumas evoke adaptive and maladaptive defensive responses and can permanently affect a given patient's defensive alignment against death. Many aspects of the conflicts and unconscious perceptions aroused by death-related triggering events remain unresolved. Existential death anxieties are intensified, and conscious and especially unconscious guilt (e.g. survivor guilt or guilt over death wishes against a deceased or damaged individual) are activated. These forces combine to harden the patient's defensive alignment against death anxiety so that his or her emotion-processing mind makes use of more extensive and often intractable communicative, psychological, and behavioural defences than before the trauma. Defensive denial and communicative obliteration become especially strong.

5. *The tendency of patients to prefer modified therapeutic frames and to avoid secured frames.* Design features of the emotion-processing mind and psychodynamic factors cause patients to prefer (and to be offered by their therapists) compromised or frame-deviant settings and ground rules for their psychotherapies. This, in turn, favours the use of obliterating mental defences and actions that preclude or diminish communication of encoded meaning related to death issues.

On the other hand, patients and therapists tend to avoid secured frames to avoid the experience of secured-frame death anxieties—and with that, the possibility of their insightful resolution. These defensive frame modifications interfere with the direct and encoded working over of death-related triggering events and their eventual deep unconscious interpretation.

6. *The critical role played by therapists' interventions in activating death anxieties.* The overuse of resistances and defences against the expression and exploration of death-related issues is prompted by the fact that patients' deep unconscious systems respond almost exclusively to triggers constituted by the interventions of their therapists—in particular, frame managements and self-revelations related to illness, injury, and death.

Patients tend consciously and unconsciously to be protective of their therapists. They are quite uncomfortable not only with direct confrontations with therapists regarding hurtful interventions, but in expressing hurtful encoded perceptions of the therapists' errant ways. Similarly, their need to idealize their therapists prompts them defensively to avoid acknowledging both conscious and unconscious perceptions of their healer's illnesses or injuries.

These defensive attitudes and communicative tendencies are unconsciously reinforced by therapists' own general resistances against working over insightfully their patients' valid unconscious perceptions of their damaging errors. At times of vulnerability, therapists also prefer deviant to secured frames, and therefore unwittingly discourage and fail to attend to encoded directives to maintain the ground rules of therapy. Thus, anxieties and defences within both patients and therapists mitigate against open and especially encoded expressions of patients' deep unconscious experiences of their therapists' efforts and revelations—the very arena where the most profound death anxieties need to be revealed and resolved.

SUMMING UP

There are, then, many factors that make meaningful therapeutic work with death-related issues very difficult, especially at the level of deep unconscious experience. In contrast, there are surprisingly few factors that make this work easier by enabling therapists and patients to counteract the massive defensive forces that interfere with these efforts. Trigger-decoding is the key to these countermeasures and to gaining access to the critical deep unconscious experiences patients and therapists naturally defend themselves against.

Death with its accoutrements appears to be one of the most difficult aspects of psychotherapy—and of human life as well. Yet here too there is a trade-off: while fraught with psychological danger, there is no more healing experience in psychotherapy than the insightful mastery of death anxieties and the development of the ability to welcome, tolerate, and benefit from secured frames.

CHAPTER FOUR

Death issues in the clinical situation

To sharpen the clinical sense of how death issues materialize in and affect the course of a psychotherapy experience, I turn now to a brief clinical excerpt.

Dr Denton is a male psychotherapist who works within a psychoanalytic framework. His patient, Mrs Peters, is a woman in her mid-thirties who came to therapy for repeated episodes of depression.

A year into the therapy and three weeks before Dr Denton was due to take a month off for his summer vacation, Mrs Peters suffered and described in her session several recent traumatic incidents. Her father had fallen ill with a serious heart attack; he was in the hospital and near death, but surviving. There had been bitter arguments with her husband because he had had to travel for business and the patient felt deserted at her time of need. The patient was also distressed because her 14-year-old daughter had been out late, and the patient had fantasied that she had been killed in a car accident. When her daughter finally returned home, Mrs Peters, with uncharacteristic loss of control, had hit her daughter rather severely.

In her sessions, Mrs Peters consciously worked over her reactions to her father's illness. She spoke of her ambivalence towards him, of fears that he would die and that her mother would become a burden to her, and of her resentment because he kept his distance from her. Then, in her penultimate session before her therapist's vacation, she made an unusual request of him. She asked that, in light of her severe distress, Dr Denton give her a telephone number where she could reach him while he was away. She assured him that she would call him only in case of a dire emergency.

Her appeal was explored in that session and the following one, largely in terms of the patient's manifest thoughts and associations, which centred on her fears of harming her daughter and her feeling that she was falling apart and had no one to turn to for support and to help reinforce her failing controls. Dr Denton simply indicated that he would think about her request and let her know his decision the following week.

In the session before Dr Denton was to leave, Mrs Peters recalled a strange incident that had happened some ten years earlier. She had gone on a summer holiday trip with her husband, and when they reached their destination and opened the trunk of their car, they discovered that their dog had somehow got into the trunk and had suffocated because of the extreme heat. Mrs Peters had arranged for a house sitter to feed the dog, which, she thought, had been left at home. Her husband had packed the boot, so she was quite furious with him for not seeing the animal and getting him out of the car. In the session, she connected this memory to the travelling she was doing to see her father and to her therapist's vacation, during which he, too, was likely to be on some kind of a trip.

Dr Denton offered the interpretation that Mrs Peters was concerned that while he was away, some disaster would befall her, and possibly her father or himself. He also mentioned possible death wishes against himself because he was deserting Mrs

Peters at a time of great need. She responded by confessing that she knew very little about herself and her needs. She acknowledged that death certainly was something she feared, but she did not want to be a murderer. She then asked again if she could have the phone number that she had requested. Dr Denton, who felt anxious about his patient's loss of control and sense of depression and was concerned about abandoning her at a time of extreme vulnerability, complied with her request.

The patient did not call Dr Denton during his vacation. In her first session on his return, she indicated that her father was still alive but remained physically disabled. She then reported a dream of *a man who was trying to kidnap her. She found him attractive but fought him off nonetheless.*

In associating to the dream, Mrs Peters recalled a teenage memory of an uncle and aunt who had taken her with them on a summer holiday soon after the death of the uncle's mother—the patient's grandmother—only to have the uncle attempt to seduce her. She had never trusted this uncle, and she should not have risked going away with him—she was angry with herself for doing so. She hoped he would die and rot in hell with guilt over what he did, especially because it happened so soon after the death of his dear mother.

THE TRADITIONAL FORMULATION

The patient

I will first offer a formulation of this material that a conventional analytically oriented therapist might well make on the basis of the manifest material and its implications. The key issues for this patient would be seen as the illness of her father, the conflicts with her husband, her loss of control with her daughter, and the impending vacation of her therapist. Among these issues, the serious illness of her father is the clearest death-connected event. In addition, the therapist's vacation is the kind of intervention (broadly defined) that symbolically and with minimal disguise is connected with death through the themes of separation and loss.

Both of these issues evoked *conscious conflicts* in the patient, which were expressed in the session in terms of her ambivalent feelings towards her father, her anger towards him for his unavailability to her during her childhood, and her anxious concern that he would die. There were also indications of manifest separation anxiety in the patient, as reflected in her request for her therapist's vacation telephone number.

There were signs of (*superficial*) *unconscious conflict* as well. Via the use of minimal displacement and disguise (the invocation of thinly encoded derivatives), these conflicts and their attendant anxieties were expressed in the story of the death of the dog. The tale encodes the loss of both the father and the therapist. But the story might also well represent unconscious death wishes towards both men—in a sense, the husband had killed the dog—and responsive guilt for these wishes.

Both the manifest exploration of the patient's conflicts and the interpretation of her repressed and disguised fears and wishes primarily involve the workings of the conscious system of the emotion-processing mind and its superficial unconscious subsystem. The conscious system operates in terms of: (1) the directly conveyed and implied meanings of a patient's material, and (2) the unconscious processing of underlying conflicts that are reflected in thinly disguised narrative images and themes. Thus, the system deals with the evident implications of death and death-related events. The hallmarks of these efforts are their generalities and their rather evident representations (barely disguised and undisguised) and meanings. (In contrast, the deep unconscious system deals with very specific triggering events and their definitive unconsciously perceived meanings. These are revealed through heavily disguised derivatives whose trigger-decoding—that is, deciphering in light of particular events—generates surprising and unexpected—non-evident—insights.)

Some therapists would also suggest that "in the transference relationship" the patient was expressing through displacement and disguise an unconscious fantasy that her therapist's departure was a form of death, and they might add that she was responding to this with unconscious death wishes and feelings of guilt. Some of this postulated murderous rage could also be a reaction to her husband's violence. Her own fury, whatever its sources, seems to have been displaced onto and expressed with her daughter.

Associations to her father's violent temper and to his frequent business trips seem to provide a personal genetic link to these experiences and to illuminate further the patient's reaction to these consciously known trigger events within her therapy and outside it. The dream and associations in the session after Dr Denton's holiday may be formulated along similar lines, as reflecting additional transference-based unconscious fantasies of joining Dr Denton and his wife on their vacation, and of winning the oedipal rivalry with his wife by seducing her therapist.

This, then, is a sampling of one possible classical analytic formulation of the patient's material, and it may well have some validity (but compare with below).

The therapist

The therapist's decision to provide his vacation telephone number to his patient raises issues related to two of the basic ground rules of therapy. The first calls for the relative anonymity of the therapist, who is obliged to refrain from personal self-revelations. The second states that the contact between patient and therapist should be confined to the time and place of the sessions.

The position that a conventional therapist takes on the management of these ground rules depends on his or her clinical orientation regarding the general principles that guide the handling of the ground rules or frame of psychotherapy (see chapter 13). However, these standard viewpoints are based on attending to patients' manifest material and its evident implications, reflections of the operations of the conscious system. This system and conscious thinking are relatively frame-insensitive, rather inconsistent in their position, and inclined towards modifying rather than securing the ground rules of therapy—supporting these unconsciously driven needs with abundant rationalizations. Frame-securing efforts by patients (and their therapists) are quite rare.

As a result of these factors, the evaluations by conventional therapists of Dr Denton's modifications of these two ground rules of this therapy are likely to lack a consensus. Some therapists would support Dr Denton's decision to give the patient his telephone number, justifying it as a necessary and innocuous departure from the usual rules of therapy because the patient was in a severe crisis. They would see this gesture as an empathic act and propose that failure to respond in this way would be experienced by the patient as unempathic and a hostile rejection.

Other manifest-content, dynamically oriented therapists would see this deviation as infantalizing the patient and creating an over-dependence on the therapist; they would be critical of what he did. Little could be done to decide definitively which viewpoint is more valid. Conscious-system discussions of therapists' interventions are seldom, if ever, conclusive.

THE COMMUNICATIVE FORMULATION

The conscious-system response

The adaptation-oriented communicative approach, which is described in coming chapters, formulates critical aspects of this material quite differently. With its stress on the mind's adaptation to specific triggering events, the approach considers both conscious and deep unconscious levels of coping. The former operates through both conscious and superficially unconscious efforts at adaptation, while the latter operates solely through deeply unconscious adaptive responses.

Clinically, conscious-system adaptive efforts tend to be both direct (and manifestly reported) and indirect or displaced (and reported *through thinly disguised narrative images*). Deep-unconscious-system adaptive efforts operate entirely outside awareness and are reflected in heavily disguised, displaced, and encoded narrative tales.

To some extent, communicative formulations of the activities of the conscious system overlap with standard proposals, though the communicative efforts tend to be more specifically organized around the unconscious meanings of activating triggering events and to focus on the primacy of the interventions of the therapist far more than incidents that occur outside therapy. In addition, communicative propositions emphasize *unconscious experience and perception,* affording conscious and unconscious fantasies and memories a credible but secondary place in human adaptive efforts (mainly as influences on the personally selective nature of what is perceived and the meanings ascribed to it).

For patients in psychotherapy—and their therapists—the adaptation-evoking triggering events to which the conscious system responds involve occurrences both inside and outside therapy. Death-related incidents evoke conscious death anxieties and activate conscious and superficially unconscious motives that determine direct and displaced reactions to the event. This level of unconscious displacement is especially prevalent within therapists because they tend to displace their unconscious reactions to personal death-related experiences from their outside lives into their work with their patients (see below). In contrast, the deep unconscious system is activated almost exclusively by events within a psychotherapy. For patients, the triggers are the interventions of their therapists, while for therapists, their deep unconscious responses are adaptive reactions to patients' communications and behaviours.

While the conscious system reacts to a wide range of triggering events, the deep unconscious system is far more selective in its perceptive scope and is mainly responsive to events (interventions and behaviours) that involve frames, rules, and boundaries (see chapter 13). Both frame-securing and frame-modifying interventions prompt patients to generate highly disguised, encoded narrative images that embody their unconscious perception of these triggers, their meanings, and patients' frame-management recommendations—which always speak for securing altered frames.

The definition of this level of deeply unconscious perception and experience requires the process of *trigger-decoding*. This requires a full appreciation of the nature of the adaptation-evoking triggering event—in this case, the therapist's frame break. With this as the guide, the patient's narrative themes are then lifted from their manifest context and placed into the context of the frame-related triggering event. The themes are formulated as personally selected, valid unconscious perceptions of the meanings of the frame-altering trigger. They will also encode unconsciously expressed recommendations as to how the frame deviation could and should have been best or most adaptively handled.

* * *

We have already reviewed Mrs Peters' conscious reasons for asking for Dr Denton's telephone number and her manifest response to his doing so. We turn now to her unconscious motives and responses, beginning with her superficial unconscious reasons. As noted, we will seek this level of motivation in events that arose both in her therapy and in her outside life.

In this regard, the most powerful adaptation-evoking trigger in her day-to-day life was the life-threatening illness of her father—an obvious source of death anxiety. Patients (and their therapists) characteristically respond to potential or actual loss situations with efforts to modify rules and boundaries outside, and especially within, therapy. This tendency to break rules is a way of attempting to override the fundamental existential rule that death inexorably follows life. These efforts serve as a fantasied yet unconsciously believed means of denying the utter helplessness and anxiety evoked by the inevitability of death.

Many frame breaks provide unconsciously orchestrated forms of merger with others as a way of undoing the sense of loss and separateness that impacts on the psyche at such moments. As a rule these efforts at psychological fusion are displaced from the person who is at risk of dying to someone else. This displacement is found in the present vignette in the shift Mrs Peters made from her father to her therapist.

Frame-breaking requests or actions in response to activated death anxieties are always costly and maladaptive. They involve extremes of denial, repression, and obliteration of meaning that interfere with effecting more suitable and appropriate adaptations. The unconscious displacements that are involved tend to be extreme and result in behaviours that usually have detrimental consequences. The adaptation-evoking problem is bypassed and remains unresolved, and, in addition, the frame break (an action) interferes with the communication of decodable narrative material (a non-action form of encoded communicative expression).

In this clinical situation, Mrs Peters failed to deal adequately with the threat of losing her father and defended herself against her death anxiety by obtaining a frame deviation from her therapist. In addition, the patient displaced her anger at her father onto her husband and daughter, who suffered the patient's unconscious rage at her father for the threat that he might die—itself a major frame change. Such displaced actions will not enable the patient to resolve the death anxieties evoked by her father's illness. The failure at mastery and the patient's need for action defences are reflected in Mrs Peter's assault on her husband and daughter—a maladaptive interpersonal symptom.

The key triggering event within the therapy for the patient's conscious system was the therapist's vacation (the provision of his telephone number primarily activated the deep unconscious system; see below). The time off had been announced well in advance and was taken in a manner that is in keeping with the secured-frame ground rules of therapy, which afford the therapist the privilege of judiciously taking time out of his office. However, this aspect of the secured frame does interrupt treatment and therefore also has frame-altering aspects—*it is a secured-frame disruption of the usual frame.* As such, most of the patient's adaptive responses to this type of trigger are handled through conscious perception and are processed by the conscious system and its superficial unconscious subsystem.

These efforts at displaced, unconscious adaptation are reflected in the minimally disguised aspects of the patient's actions and narrative material. Most pertinent are the displaced themes of the threatened loss/death of her father (this allusion is both manifestly meaningful and in the service of encoded communication) and the absences of the patient's husband and daughter. These events provoked expressions of displaced anger from the patient, which, at this level, shifted the resentment from her therapist (for leaving her) to family members (her father, husband, and daughter for threatening to abandon her or actually doing so).

These actions and themes are thinly disguised displaced behaviours and allusions that pertain to the therapist's impending vacation/absence. The story of her father's brush with death and her fantasy that her daughter had been killed are the clearest reflections of the patient's superficial unconscious experience of her therapist's vacation as a death-related event. They also touch on the patient's unconsciously activated death anxieties over this impending loss.

Both the threat of losing her father and the fact that the patient's unconscious experience of, and reactions to, Dr Denton's planned vacation had gone uninterpreted in terms of deep unconscious experience played a role unconsciously in motivating Mrs Peters to ask Dr Denton to modify the ideal, secured frame. As noted, the request for his vacation telephone number violated the ground rule of relative anonymity, which requires that the therapist not make personal self-revelations to the patient. In addition, the offer of the telephone number creates the potential for additional frame modifications, in that the ideal ground rules call for the confinement of contact between patient and therapist to the time of the patient's scheduled sessions and to the therapist's professional office.

As for the patient's unconscious motives for asking for the frame deviation, the material suggests that it was intended to undo the patient's dread of loss and its conscious (father) and unconscious (therapist) elaboration as death-connected. By having the therapist's telephone number while he was away, the separation would be undone and the related death anxieties—both existential and predatory in nature—would be temporarily ameliorated. The sense of relief afforded by possessing the number appears to be one reason that the patient did not in fact need to telephone the therapist.

However, motives of this kind are never entirely intrapsychic within the patient. They are product of the therapeutic interaction and of the patient/therapist system. This kind of frame-altering maladaptive response by a patient to the temporary loss of a therapist generally arises in the presence of *prior frame breaks by the therapist*, which have set the pattern for this costly means of trying to cope with loss. Indeed, Dr Denton had on several past occasions altered the therapeutic frame of Mrs Peters' treatment.

The deep unconscious response

Once the patient had made her frame-modifying request of the therapist, her deep unconscious system was activated. Most of the critical meanings of this request (and the therapist's potential to comply with it) were perceived unconsciously rather than consciously—the two levels of perception tend to be mutually exclusive. These deep unconscious meanings were then processed unconsciously and revealed through the patient's encoded narratives.

The first indication of the activation of the deep unconscious system is seen in the characteristic split in the patient's responses to this potential (and later, actual) trigger. While consciously requesting the telephone number and grateful for being given it, unconsciously, through her encoded stories, she condemned it and viewed it in a distinctly negative light (see below).

In assessing the effects of a therapist's intervention using the communicative approach, little stock is placed in the patient's manifest assessment of the effort. Preformed clinical beliefs are also not reliable. Instead, use is made of the great resource of the patient's deep unconscious intelligence and the narratives it generates. Trigger-decoding the themes in these stories in light of the frame-modifying or frame-securing triggering events that has evoked them guides the evaluation of the situation and its unconsciously experienced meanings and implications. These narratives also provide so-*called unconscious correctives or models of rectification* of therapists' errors—encoded messages as to the optimal response to the frame-related issue.

Patients' unconscious perceptions and encoded frame-management recommendations are relatively non-defensive, incisive, and adaptively sound. Thus, when the decoding process is properly carried out and used to effect both interpretations and frame-securing efforts that obtain *encoded validation*, the result is an especially healing therapeutic effort.

In this instance, the story of the dog who unknowingly joined Mrs Peters and her husband on their vacation can be shown via trigger-decoding to represent and convey meanings about the patient's unconscious expectation that she will be given her therapist's telephone number. The decoded unconsciously conveyed themes indicate that it would be experienced as Dr Denton's way of bringing Mrs Peters along with him and his wife—that is, of not abandoning her as planned. The disguised images involve the dog, the patient, and her husband as representations of the patient, her therapist, and his wife. Additional representations of this unconscious perception of undoing the loss are evident in the story of the uncle and aunt, and the dream of the kidnap attempt.

The account of the death of the dog indicates, however, that providing the telephone number to the patient would be extremely destructive to her therapeutic progress (and to the therapist as well). That is, the death imagery is used here to portray *a devastating toxic and predatory consequence of this frame modification* as destructive to the patient and possibly fatal for the treatment situation because it is so entrapping and smothering—it constitutes a deviant-frame form of entrapment (Langs, 1992, 1995).

What, then, would have been the most optimally adaptive—technically valid and helpful—response that the therapist could have made to his patient's entreaty? If we return to Mrs Peter's material, we discover that while *consciously* she had asked for and accepted the telephone number, *unconsciously*, as seen in the encoded story of the dog, she had advised her therapist not to take her along with him—her husband should not have allowed the dog to get into the trunk of their car.

After the frame had been modified, similar advice is encoded in the dream of fighting off the attractive kidnapper (a narrative that also encodes the entrapping and criminal aspects of the rule break) and in the comment that she should not have gone along with her uncle (a story that emphasizes the seductive aspects of the frame break). The plea for punishment and feelings of guilt, and for suffering for seductively modifying the frame, completes the patient's unconscious response—as with the uncle who should rot in hell, the therapist should pay for his violation of the ground rules.

To summarize, a death-related event outside this therapy (the illness of the patient's father) joined forces with an unconsciously experienced, death-evoking, uninterpreted, frame-securing yet -modifying event within the therapy (the therapist's vacation) to create a pair of triggers that unconsciously motivated this patient's request for a frame modification from her therapist. This entreaty constituted a maladaptive effort to cope with the death anxieties that these two incidents had aroused. The power of these unconscious sources of Mrs Peters' request far outweigh the conscious reasons she offered to Dr Denton—arguments that he mistakenly took at face value and to which he therefore acceded. The patient's conscious thoughts and pleas functioned mainly as excuses or rationalizations created to justify a request that was strongly driven by unrecognized unconscious forces and needs (much as Dr Denton's acceding to the request was similarly rationalized and unconsciously driven; see below).

The patient made this appeal consciously and then based her actual behaviour, her coping response, on these conscious needs. Even though her deep unconscious wisdom system spoke strongly of the harmful effects of this deviant request and advised the therapist and herself via derivative (encoded) imagery not to do it, this system's sound encoded insights did not affect her actual approach to the situation. In her behavioural efforts at adaptation, she continued to ask for the telephone number. Thus, consciously, the patient saw the offer of the telephone number as a concerned and kindly act, but deeply unconsciously she viewed it as murderous, seductive, criminal, and quite out of line.

In regard to therapeutic technique, Dr Denton's more appropriate response to the patient's request would have been to use the expectation that he would comply with the patient's appeal—an anticipated trigger (Langs, 1992)—as the basis for trigger-decoding her story of the dog, including its frame-securing directive. He could thereby have interpreted the encoded meanings of her narratives, including her own unconscious advice as to how to deal with the frame issue she had raised. This advice was encoded in the allusion to leaving the dog (the patient) at home, and it reflects, of course, the secured-frame solution. On this basis, Dr Denton would not have provided Mrs Peters with the telephone number, doing so in accordance with her own encoded recommendations. She thereby would have benefited from his interpretative understanding and his capacity to hold the frame securely.

The therapist's unconscious motives

This brings us to the therapist and a final question: Why did Dr Denton acquiesce to his patient's frame-altering request? Was he, too, under the sway of unconscious death-related forces of which he was quite unaware?

There are two indicators that Dr Denton could have noticed that would have led him to suspect that countertransferences were involved in his thoughts of revealing his telephone number to Mrs Peters. The first was that this was the first time he had ever thought of participating in a deviation of this kind. The inclination to make an unusual intervention is a signal for both restraint and self-processing (the communicative version of so-called self-analysis; Langs, 1993). Before invoking an intervention of that kind, a therapist should first search for pathological unconscious motives, including needs that involve death anxiety.

The second indicator of likely countertransferences is a basic principle of technique that applies to all cases: *Every frame modification by a therapist, whether requested by a patient or volunteered by the therapist, has a strong and critical countertransference aspect to it and is always maladaptive. Such an intervention is driven by pathological motives, among which an unconscious attempt to deal with conscious and/or unconscious sources of unresolved death anxiety is quite prominent.*

Frames are best kept secured, and self-exploration is best carried out before deviating—the impulse to modify a ground rule is a cue to constrain and self-explore. Once a frame modification has been invoked, it is the therapist's responsibility to discover the specific unconscious conflicts and death-related issues that have motivated the deviant intervention. These efforts are, however, the private responsibility of the therapist, and the patient should not be burdened with any aspect of these endeavours.

Direct speculation and intellectual analyses are inadequate for this purpose because they confine the search to the realm of conscious experience and adapting. The far more powerful deeply unconscious motives and adaptive efforts that empower these actions cannot be articulated by this means. More complex self-processing is needed (Langs, 1993).

The therapist must allow himself or herself, in private, to generate a pool of narrative themes and seek out a death-related adaptation-evoking triggering event that gives deep meaning to these images and which accounts unconsciously for the deviation. On this basis, he or she is in a position to hold the frame secured and correctly self-interpret the various meanings of the inclination to deviate. Almost always, the death-related event that is activating the therapist's unmastered death anxieties lies within his own life—personal or in terms of a direct experience with a patient (i.e. a patient's illness, injury or death).

Frame modifications are the primary enacted means through which both patients and therapists attempt to adapt to unresolved death anxieties. A therapist's inclination to modify a ground rule or actually altering one calls for the private search for death-connected triggering events in his or her life—within and/or outside therapy.

Similarly, if a deviation is enacted, self-processing can be used to discover the therapist's triggers and motives for doing so. This places the therapist in the best possible position subsequently to use the patient's material for validated interpretations and efforts to rectify the frame as much as possible. While harmful to some extent, frame modifications also can serve the therapeutic process if they are recognized and soundly handled.

In this clinical example, the death-related serious illness of Mrs Peters' father was not likely to trigger Dr Denton's deep unconscious death anxieties unless the situation resonated with a personal death-related issue of his own. Similarly, a death-related incident that arises in the therapy of another patient will have the power to evoke displaced death-defending deviations in the situation with Mrs Peters only if that event touches on death-related conflicts within the therapist. It follows, then, that Dr Denton must search for a personal death-related triggering event to account for his frame deviations.

At times, the key event has been set to the side and repressed, and there must be an intensive search for the missing trigger (encoded themes are a valuable clue). At other times, the triggering event is within conscious awareness, but its most compelling unconscious meanings and the unresolved death anxieties they have aroused, and the link to the frame deviation, are quite unconscious.

Death-related triggering events in a therapist's life operate as deeply unconscious sources of deviant interventions. The death-related meanings of these triggering events are unconsciously perceived and processed, and they are then encoded in the therapist's self-processing narratives. The themes in these stories must be properly trigger-decoded to yield essential insights into the deeply unconscious basis for these actions.

Life events experienced by psychotherapists greatly affect how they work, intervene, and manage the frameworks of the therapies they offer to their patients. For everyone, including psychotherapists, experiences of loss are linked to death and dying, and they breed denial-based, communication-obliterating frame deviations.

The therapist's trigger

When he subjected this interlude to self-processing, Dr Denton eventually discovered the key triggering event for his frame-modifying decision. Just three weeks earlier, his sister had died of a brain tumour, and he now realized that he was still immersed in the mourning process. Her death had unconsciously prompted his frame break through which he, via displacement, denied her loss and his own helplessness in the face of his sister's fatal illness.

The offer of his telephone number to his patient was his displaced and maladaptive way of dealing with the unresolved death anxieties that this disaster had caused him. Secondarily, then, the death anxieties that his patient had aroused in him, which were linked unconsciously to the loss of his sister, overloaded the adaptive capacities of his emotion-processing mind and prompted an action form of discharge rather than a more contemplative, thoughtful response to his patient's request.

Dr Denton's selection of Mrs Peters for his displaced, defensive, denial-based, communication-disrupting frame modification is maladaptive and harmful to both himself and his patient. The act cannot, of course, undo the loss of his sister. Nor did it lessen his death anxieties. Instead, because he will unconsciously perceive the harm it causes his patient and will experience deep unconscious guilt, the deviation is likely to intensify his anxieties and conflicts over his sister's death. His survival and other forms of guilt related to the loss of his sister also will not be resolved in this manner. Unconsciously, he is likely to invite punishment from the patient as payment for his real and imagined hurts to his sister and his real hurts of the patient. This intention seems to have been unconsciously detected by Mrs Peters, who encoded this perception in the story of her uncle towards whom she wished all manner of punishments, including death.

In this light, we can see that the death themes in Mrs Peters' material—the dead dog and the deceased grandmother—represent her unconscious appreciation that death-related experiences and anxieties had motivated Dr Denton to agree to modify the frame as he did. Both images reflect unconscious perceptions of the role that death played in the anticipated and then actual offer of the telephone number. Strikingly, the later story of the uncle decodes to imply that the loss of his mother had prompted his attempt to violate a social frame and rule, and to try to seduce his niece (the patient). Unconsciously, the patient seems to have appreciated that her therapist's frame alterations were invoked in a desperate and failed attempt to cope with both loss and death anxiety.

When a therapist modifies the ground rules of therapy, the patient will experience the unconscious meanings of the deviation via unconscious perception and processing, and will try unconsciously to comprehend both its nature and its sources in the therapist (efforts that are all but impossible and seldom made consciously). When sensing countertransference, therapists may turn to their patients' material for clues to the active unconscious triggers for, and meanings of, their errant efforts. But a therapist's definitive search for insight is not part of his assigned task in psychotherapy, and such pursuits during a patient's sessions should be quickly attenuated and later on carried forward privately.

Nevertheless, a patient's unconscious processing of his or her therapist's interventions is a resource that should not be entirely ignored by the therapist. The deep unconscious wisdom system, a kind of *deep unconscious ego* that creates and encodes the patient's narrative tales, has an *emotional intelligence* that far exceeds that of the conscious mind. This information can be put to good use by the therapist if it is noticed quickly and concentration is returned to the patient's material and needs. In any case, the information available to the patient is vast but limited by the information and clues that can be sensed unconsciously. Ultimately, the therapist must do his or her own self-processing to discover the specific events—and their unconscious meanings—that have triggered an errant intervention, so corrective measures can be taken as needed.

The patient's allusion to the death of the dog in the trunk of her car is a rather typical representation of the anxiety-provoking aspects of a secured frame. This type of frame is experienced unconsciously as a safe and supportive space, but also as a space that is closed and entrapping and therefore connected to death and dreaded. The image encodes both the therapist's and the patient's fears of the secured frame, and both sets of fears would need to be interpreted—and rectification carried out accordingly. Regarding the telephone number, the best the therapist could do when he resumed sessions is to use the patient's material to assure her that he would not give her his number again. He might then have to pass a later test of this resolve in order for the patient to be convinced of his frame-securing intentions. This is the only sound way that this unconscious frame-modifying and maladaptive therapeutic misalliance could be eliminated.

Finally, note that the seductive aspects of this frame alteration were operating in the service of the denial of loss and death. A great deal of unconsciously motivated seductive and sexual behaviour, especially when it is rule-breaking, is invoked to deny, and thereby maladaptively respond to, death anxieties. There are many complexities to how we experience and adapt to death issues; understanding these intricacies will clarify many puzzling therapeutic interludes and enable therapists to comprehend and rectify many untoward therapeutic moments.

SOME BASIC PERSPECTIVES

Some basic perspectives on death and death anxiety are relevant to this clinical material; some clarify earlier points and others introduce fresh insights:

1. For humans, death is a universal adaptive issue and a cause for anxiety which may be experienced consciously and/or unconsciously.
2. Conscious death anxiety is experienced manifestly and directly.
   a. In most instances, this form of death anxiety is triggered by an actual, impending, or recent death event, illness, injury, and the like—in either self or others.
   b. Manageable conscious concerns and thoughts about death may well prove to be adaptive.
   c. Excessive worry or obsessively thinking about death speaks for maladaptation.
   d. The extreme form of unmanaged death anxiety may be termed "mortophobia"—an excessive, phobic fear of death and dying.
      i. Fears of being buried alive and claustrophobic symptoms are dysfunctional consequences of unresolved death anxiety.
3. Unconscious death anxiety operates without direct awareness and can be recognized in two ways:
   a. Through behaviours that speak for its presence—this includes manic actions, frame modifications, and uncontrolled, frame-breaking, and perverse sexuality.
   b. Through encoded narrative communications—given a death-related triggering event, the stories told by patients (and in self-processing, by therapists) will involve themes of death; such narratives speak for unconscious death anxiety whose sources and activating triggers must then be discovered.
4. Conscious and unconscious death anxieties are issues for both patient and therapist throughout a given psychotherapy. However, these issues will be especially intense when a death-related triggering event takes place—in the therapy itself and/or in the life of the patient and/or the therapist.
5. Phenomenologically, there are three pertinent classifications of death anxieties:

a. *Type*—existential versus traumatic–toxic–predatory.

b. *Who is involved*—primary (regarding self) versus secondary (regarding others).

c. *Duration*—immediate and recent (acute) versus remote and long-standing (chronic).

6. The triggers that activate death anxieties are of two main types:

   a. Triggers manifestly or evidently linked to death—*the damage package*—illness, injury, separation, loss, physical and psychological assaults, and other blatant traumas.

   b. Triggers latently or unconsciously linked to death—primarily frame-related interventions—securing or modifying.

7. The identification of the triggers that bring forth death-related themes is crucial for understanding the nature of the underlying problems and their effects. Without the trigger, the death-related imagery floats in the air, so to speak, and can be explored solely and with severe limitations in terms of conscious experience. When linked together, triggers and narrative themes can reveal much about the deep unconscious experience of death-related issues.

8. There are, then:

   a. Consciously recognized death-related triggering events: the manifest meanings and implications of these incidents are worked over consciously, while the additional latent, repressed, and denied meanings are processed by the deep unconscious system, outside direct awareness; these latter meanings can be accessed only through trigger-decoding.

   b. Unconsciously recognized death-related triggering events, in response to which all of the processing is carried out in the deep unconscious system, without conscious knowledge: the result is a wide range of displaced actions and symptoms, and encoded images whose meanings can be discovered—again—only through trigger-decoding.

   The search for repressed, so-called missing triggers is a critical part of the psychotherapeutic work pertaining to death-related conflicts and syndromes.

9. Every individual has a preferred means of adapting to death-

related issues—these adaptive efforts are strikingly defensive in nature; death anxiety is a major motive for the defensive operations of all patients and therapists. These coping strategies have four sources:

a. The evolved design of the emotion-processing mind. These are hard-wired, inherited psychological resources and defences that are extremely difficult to modify. They are characteristic of our species and are shared by all humans—though in an individually characteristic manner (individual differences constrained by a common or universal structure).
b. The specific details of a given person's death-related trauma history.
c. Mental defences and resources that have developed over a given individual's lifetime. These developmental resources are greatly affected by psychodynamic factors such as relationships, self-preservative needs, conflicts, cooperation, sexual and aggressive needs, perceptions of others (conscious and unconscious), and especially the aforementioned trauma or death-related history of the person.
d. The unique qualities of death as an adaptation-evoking triggering event and danger situation. The ultimate irresolvability of death powerfully shapes the adaptive efforts and defences that are mobilized against the anxieties it evokes.

10. Because they can never fully succeed in defending against death, humans have developed only one fundamental psychological defence against death anxiety—that of denial. This basic defence comes in many forms and gradations and is supplemented by a variety of additional psychological and action types of defences:
    a. In the realm of *communication*, the main defences are of three kinds:
        i. Communicative obliteration and non-communication.
        ii. The natural use of encoding or disguise.
        iii. Failures to carry out the steps needed to trigger-decode encoded narratives.

11. There is a critical syndrome that is produced by repeated exposure to death-related events or by an especially intense single experience of this kind—for example, the suicide of a parent. It is called *the syndrome of adaptive failure caused by over-intense exposure to death-related traumas* (Langs, 1992). Patients (and therapists) suffering from this syndrome are terrified both of secured frames and of death-related images and their meanings, even when they are encoded. Their mental defences against death anxiety on all levels are extremely obliterating and action-oriented, and they are very difficult to alter.

12. Death-related experiences have a profound effect on the emotion-processing mind and on the way it processes and adapts to all types of emotionally charged trigger events—including, but not limited to, those that are death-related. In general, death-linked traumas greatly intensify the defensive alignment and processing strategies of the emotion-processing mind, creating a wide range of maladaptive and difficult-to-modify denial-based psychological, communicative, and behavioural defences (Langs, 1995).

* * *

It can be said, then, that both living and doing psychotherapy are difficult issues, and that death is an all but impossible aspect of both. We need to find the means of making death-related concerns, conscious and unconscious, more tolerable to us as therapists and to our patients. Adapt well to death by arriving at a deep and nondefensive form of acceptance and/or resignation in both the world at large and in the domain of psychotherapy, and you are assured of a more satisfying and healthier life—and when the time comes, death as well.

CHAPTER FIVE

Observing and formulating

The communicative approach, and its particular means of observing and formulating the transactions of the therapeutic interaction, is the basis for the ideas presented in this volume (Langs, 1982, 1988, 1992, 1993, 1995). I will therefore briefly present the essentials of its methods as they pertain to the study of death and the anxieties it arouses.

COMMUNICATIVE FORMULATIONS

The communicative approach is a significant departure from the standard model, which is based, in essence, on a weak adaptive position and is focused in the manifest contents of patients' material, their evident implications in terms of fantasies, wishes, and needs, and their personal genetic connections (Langs, 1992, 1993). In contrast, the communicative approach is based on a strong adaptive and interpersonal viewpoint of the patient as a human being who copes on two levels—one attached to awareness (i.e.

consciously) and the other entirely without direct awareness (i.e. unconsciously). Thus, communication is both conscious and unconscious, direct (unencoded) and disguised (encoded).

The communicative mode of listening and formulating can be characterized as follows:

1. Manifest meanings and their implications are recognized and assessed as expressions of the operations of *the conscious system of the emotion-processing mind*. These meanings are reflections of:
    a. The patient's conscious concerns, feelings, perceptions, fantasies, and known behaviours activated in response to known adaptive issues. At this level, they involve conscious coping strategies.
    b. The adaptation-evoking experiences that the patient copes with via the superficial unconscious system. These issues and their processing are reflected in thinly disguised encoded narrative communications—for example, a story about a professor who is late to class which encodes a therapist's lateness to a recent session.
2. The most compelling form of latent or unconscious meaning is taken to be *heavily encoded in the manifest narratives or stories* told by patients in the course of their sessions. These displaced and disguised *derivative messages* reflect unconscious adaptive responses to repressed triggers and to the repressed meanings of known triggers.
3. Encoded messages are created and imparted by the second basic system of the emotion-processing mind—*the deep unconscious system.*
    a. Inputs reach this mental module by means of *unconscious perception*. They are then processed, without awareness interceding, by means of a deep unconscious intelligence—*the deep unconscious wisdom subsystem*, an adaptive resource of great sensitivity and capability.
    b. Because unconscious perception deals with highly disturbing and anxiety-provoking meanings, the deep unconscious system is, by design, incapable of revealing its perceptions and processing efforts directly to awareness. The system's

efforts reach consciousness solely through *encoded stories*—disguise is always present.

c. The deep unconscious system deals with repressed aspects of triggers. Searching for adaptation-evoking experiences that are not registered consciously is vital to accessing the experiences of this system and its adaptive efforts.

d. Because the workings of the deep unconscious wisdom subsystem are unconscious, the adaptive insights generated by this system are not directly available to awareness and do not affect direct, conscious efforts at adaptation. That is, the deep unconscious wisdom subsystem influences human *communication*, mainly its narrative messages, but has virtually no influence over human *behaviour*. Trigger-decoding is the essential means of making deep unconscious insights available for use in conscious adaptation.

f. The second subsystem of the deep unconscious system, *the fear/guilt subsystem*, embodies both unconscious guilt and unconscious fears of death. This subsystem affects a patient's encoded communications in therapy, but its main effects are symptomatic and behavioural (see chapter 6). Because this subsystem has a powerful but unconscious influence on adaptation and behaviour, emotional adaptation is skewed towards denial of death and self-punishment.

5. Access to the anxieties, conflicts, insights, and adaptive recommendations of the deep unconscious system can be gained only through *trigger-decoding*. This process calls for a search for critical triggering events and their most compelling meanings, and the linking of these triggers to the extracted themes contained in a patient's narrative images. The results of this linking are formulated in terms of unconscious perception, experience, processing, and adaptive recommendations. Unconscious fantasy formations are seen as secondary reactions to reality events that are consciously or unconsciously perceived and processed.

   Deep insight is available only through trigger-decoding.

6. The stress in the communicative approach is on unconscious experience and coping—on reality and perception more than, but not excluding, fantasy and imagination. Personal genetic

links, which do indeed have considerable significance, are called forth only when conveyed in the patient's material. These connections may be transparent and therefore directly retrievable and an aspect of conscious-system functioning, or they may be encoded and available only through trigger-decoding.

7. With death-related events, a surprisingly large segment of what is experienced registers subliminally or unconsciously, and it is processed in the deep unconscious system without awareness interceding. These experienced meanings are not revealed directly, but are conveyed through encoded narrative tales.
    a. The most significant aspects of a patient's death-related experiences are deeply unconscious and can therefore be ascertained only by identifying the relevant adaptation-evoking trigger events and linking the death-related and other themes in a patient's narrative material to these triggers.

The deep unconscious experience of death-related triggering events is a powerful determinant of human emotional behaviour. However, access to this level of experience is possible only through sound, validated efforts at trigger-decoding.

Illustrating the communicative approach

To illustrate the communicative approach, I offer a vignette that involves a frame-securing moment. The vignette demonstrates how trigger-decoding illuminates the unconscious aspects of death anxiety.

> Ms Potter was in empowered psychotherapy—a form of communicative psychotherapy that enhances the communication of narrative material and the search for adaptation-evoking triggers (Langs, 1993). Her therapist was Dr Travis, a woman psychologist.
>
> The patient, a single woman in her early forties, felt stuck in her life. She was unhappy with her work as an art director—a job she had held for 20 years—and she tended to suffer from intermittent episodes of morbid anxiety. The anxiety had in-

tensified some five years earlier when her sister, her only sibling, died in a car accident after leaving Ms Potter, with whom she had quarrelled—her car had been hit head-on by another car that had swerved into her lane on a rain-slicked, two-lane highway. The patient never resolved her belief that had she not argued with her, her sister would not have been killed. Ms Potter had developed a fear that she, too, would have a sudden and violent death.

Now in her second year of therapy, Ms Potter seldom spoke of her sister. She had, from time to time, mentioned her death and her feelings of guilt, but the images were flat and seemed to go nowhere. The issues surrounding the death of her sister remained unresolved.

Ms Potter began a session by mentioning that she had learned that Dr Travis was going to give a lecture on anxiety and depression at a local club to which the patient belonged. She had decided to attend the lecture because she wanted to know more about her own maladies—a little extra help would be welcome. Besides, she had read a magazine article on anxiety written by Dr Travis and had found it helpful; the lecture would only prove to be more illuminating.

The patient then reported a brief dream in which *her cousin, Belle, is with her in a small plane, which Belle is flying*. Among her narrative guided associations [associations that arise from the specific dream images] was a recollection of an air show Ms Potter had attended as a child, in which a plane had crashed and the pilot was killed. She wished she had not gone with her father to see the planes.

Ms Potter also recalled a time as an early adolescent when Belle had lost the money her mother had given them to go to the cinema. They had tried to sneak in through an exit door, but they were caught, and their parents were called by the manager of the movie theatre. It was terribly humiliating. It seemed ridiculous to do something that actually broke the law.

This vignette contains both an active frame-related *triggering event* from the therapist and an active frame-related *patient indicator*. The latter is a term for indications from the patient of an expression of psychopathology or maladaptation, usually in the form of an intrapsychic or interpersonal symptom or an effort to modify the ground rules of therapy. It is thereby an indication that the patient is in need of an interpretation or frame-securing intervention from the therapist.

The *trigger* is the announcement of the therapist's lecture. This is a frame-deviant self-revelation via a third party. The announcement also breaches the secured frame by rendering the therapist available for possible contact with the patient outside her office, at a time other than the patient's sessions. The *patient indicator*, which had been prompted by the trigger, is of course, the patient's announced frame-modifying plan to attend her therapist's lecture. This act would violate the aforementioned ground rule that states that contact between patient and therapist is confined to the therapist's office at the time of the patient's sessions. It would also violate the implied ground rule that the therapist's communications to the patient should be confined to those that are based on the patient's material in sessions and that the therapist not make personal self-revelations.

The patient's conscious adaptive response to the frame-deviant trigger of the announced lecture was her frame-deviant decision to attend—frame modifications by therapists beget frame modifications from patients. The patient also consciously rationalized her decision but, as is typical of these interactions, had little else to say about it directly.

The patient's encoded narratives must be examined and formulated to ascertain her deep unconscious perceptions of the trigger and her unconscious maladaptive response. To do this, we first *trigger-decode* Ms Potter's dream and guided associations by linking their themes to the trigger. Only then do we apply the same process to the patient's own intended frame deviation (the self-indicator).

The clinical principle is that the deep unconscious system processes and encodes unconscious perceptions of all frame-related events in psychotherapy, whether initiated by the therapist or by the patient. However, the therapist's frame-related interventions must be understood before trying to appreciate the frame-related behaviours of the patient.

The *bridging themes* that connect this imagery to the trigger are (1) viewing an air show and (2) going to the *movies*—both are themes related to seeing a performance, much as the lecture is a performance. These themes also indicate that the patient's unconscious perceptions of the deviation are those of a disaster and a voyeuristic, forbidden, criminal act. The patient also offers a model of rectification—an optimal adaptive response—in stating that she should not have attended the air show or tried to sneak into the movie theatre.

In empowered psychotherapy, patients are required to develop their own interpretations as best they can.

> The trigger-decoded interpretation and frame-management response that Ms Potter worked out was this: "I guess you'd say that my dream is telling me that I shouldn't attend the lecture because it would be a disaster and a crime. But I'm still not convinced I shouldn't go. Maybe the dream was about something else, I don't know." [This is a rather typical defensive effort of a patient that takes the form of linking her themes to the *patient indicator* rather than to the *trigger from the therapist*.]
>
> Ms Potter wondered whether there actually was another active trigger, but she failed to find one. Dr Travis then intervened: "The most immediate trigger is the announcement of my lecture, isn't it? And your imagery says it's my way of placing myself on display, and that it was disastrous of me to do it. You're also saying that I'm being dishonest in lecturing to your club, that it's my way of setting up a chance to see you under illegal conditions." [The therapist had correctly organized her comments around the *trigger* rather than the *indicator*.]
>
> Ms Potter said she could sort of see Dr Travis' point, but somehow she still wanted to go to the lecture; she couldn't see what harm it would do. She then told several additional stories that repeated the theme of illegal entry. A teenage memory also came up, in which she recalled sneaking a look at her cousin Belle in bed when they had shared a summer house; she saw her masturbating and became upset. Finally, the story of the plane crash brought to mind another incident concerning a pilot who was a friend of Belle's; he had died in a train crash.

SOME INITIAL FORMULATIONS

The theme of death appears in the patient's initial guided associations (the plane crash) and is repeated in this last association (the pilot who died in a train crash). Without the communicative approach and trigger-decoding, the first death theme might be interpreted as a symbol of the patient's voyeuristic anxieties or as reflecting some kind of violent incestuous fantasy directed against the patient's father who had taken her to the air show. Quite often, death themes are interpreted as an indication of aggressive and violent wishes and needs. While this may be the case, clinical evidence indicates that these conjectures also serve to obliterate the patient's (and therapist's) great dread of death and annihilation.

Communicative understanding adds two essential dimensions to our understanding of the appearance of these death themes in the patient's material. (1) The death themes serve to *encode* the patient's unconscious perceptions of the destructive aspects of the therapist's frame modification (the speaking engagement) and of the patient's wish to participate in the deviation. (2) Given that both deaths occurred in a confined space (the plane and train), the stories also encode the patient's unconscious perception of her therapist's and her own *secured-frame anxieties*, which are always a deeply unconscious factor in the invocation of a frame modification.

In terms of personal genetics, the underlying issue here is the death of Ms Potter's sister and the unresolved aspects of that experience for her. [To simplify the discussion, I will pass over earlier death-related traumas.] If there were no activating frame-related triggering event within the therapy, the working through of the patient's conflicts, perceptions, fantasies, thoughts, meanings, and feelings would be confined to conscious-system responses—including repressed imagery that would derive from the superficial unconscious subsystem of the conscious system. These are directly retrievable memories and fantasies with access to awareness when the repressive barrier between the superficial unconscious memory subsystem and conscious awareness is modified.

These directly recovered memories are of a different order and considerably less powerful emotionally than the repressed memories, meanings, and reactive fantasies that are locked away in the deep unconscious system's memory storage subsystem—imagery that emerges solely in encoded form in response to activating triggers within therapy. These derivatively conveyed perceptions and memories need to be trigger-decoded in order to be appreciated consciously.

There are clues in this material that this frame deviation and the possibility of its partial rectification were the patient to decide not to attend the lecture have aroused in the patient severe death anxieties related to her sister's death. They are found in the representation of the sister by the cousin and in the allusions to the plane and train crashes, which encode the means by which her sister died. Yet, despite strong efforts by Dr Travis to get Ms Potter to associate to these images, these connections did not come forth from the patient. Thus, no personal genetic interpretation could be made for the moment.

This kind of stalemate is fairly typical of situations that are connected with severe death anxieties. As long as there are active frame deviations (i.e. existing frame modifications), the patient's deep unconscious system's communicative and repressive defences will hold firm, and interpretations of deep unconscious reactions to the traumatic death-related experience are not possible. Nevertheless, in principle, the therapist should not undo or bypass a patient's repressive and communicative defences by introducing the death-related issue. Doing so leads only to rage in the patient over validly feeling assaulted and to intellectualizations that render the death-related material ineffectual.

Dr Travis was limited in what she could do for the moment. She needed to sit back and wait for a frame-securing moment—an incident in which the ground rules were maintained in the face of the patient's pressures for them to be modified. This type of intervention would alter the patient's communicative defences and make available the deep unconscious aspects of the patient's experience of the death of her sister for meaningful trigger-decoding—the material would emerge in response to the frame-securing triggering event.

One reason for the patient's deeply motivated wish to stick to her decision to go to the lecture—that is, to break the frame—was her need to defend against the emergence of the deeply unconscious meanings of the death of her sister and the powerful and terrifying affects and realizations that they would unleash. This contrasts with the more intellectualized and transparent conscious-system working over this death event. The availability of encoded derivatives and their interpretation involves powerful meanings and affects that are not accessible through direct exploration.

The vignette continued

In the following session, the patient generated additional narratives that encoded a strong unconscious directive to herself not to attend the lecture. When Dr Travis interpreted this material, thereby creating frame-securing pressures on the patient, Ms Potter produced a confirmatory encoded narrative. However, consciously, she again insisted that none of this necessarily meant that she should stay away.

In the session before the lecture was to take place, Ms Potter brought a dream in which *she is in a car with her best friend from adolescence, Grace. Suddenly, Grace, who is driving, turns the wheel of the car and it careens off the road and into a tree.* The patient feels the impact of the crash and wakes from the dream with a terrified start.

Among her guided associations to the dream elements, the patient recalled an incident in which Grace had been caught cheating on a psychology examination. The teacher who was monitoring the examination had left the room, and Grace had seized the chance to get out her book and look for answers; it was a disastrous error on her part, and she had been suspended from school.

This and other stories were decoded by Dr Travis as once again conveying the dishonesty of both the offered lecture and of the patient's insistence on attending it. The narratives suggested that it would be a disastrous error to exploit the therapist's lapse. The patient then pondered the images and themes and announced that she would not go to the lecture. Soon afterwards, Dr Travis, using the patient's encoded directives, stated that she would no longer offer lectures at the patient's club [her frame rectification].

Ms Potter's next association was to Grace's success as an artist; she had recently had a show at a prominent gallery, and her work was hanging in museums across the country. Then Ms Potter recalled that Grace had nearly been killed in a dormitory fire at college when she was trapped in her room. She was rescued at the last moment by the firemen who had responded to the fire alarm.

Somehow the fire brought to mind the fact that Grace's mother had committed suicide by jumping in front of a train. Ms Potter described the incident in some detail and recalled spending time with Grace, who had been hysterical after her mother's violent death. The mother had been depressed because Grace's father had abandoned the family and run off with a woman with whom he worked. There had been an attempt at reconciliation, but it ended in a savage quarrel. Grace's mother had run from their house to the railroad tracks and quickly ended her life.

Ms Potter's sister Carol had been a close friend of Grace's sister, and Carol also had been involved in the funeral and mourning that had ensued after the suicide. Suddenly, Ms Potter decoded the entrapment and suicide imagery as being linked to the death of her sister, and with some help from Dr Travis, the images were connected to the patient's decision to hold the frame of her therapy secured by not attending the lecture. For her part, Dr Travis used her patient's images as a basis for promising not to lecture at the patient's club in the future. [The secured-frame moment had materialized at last.]

Ms Potter suddenly remembered that right after her sister had died, she had had many upsetting nightmares about the accident. Another recollection came next. It concerned a long-forgotten comment made by the other driver in the accident, which seemed to suggest that Ms Potter's sister could have taken evasive action and avoided the accident. It was as if she had committed suicide after quarrelling with the patient, and because of that, Ms Potter felt like a murderer. She had read a newspaper story some time previously about a woman who, when she accidentally backed her car over her son and killed him, immediately locked herself into her garage and committed suicide.

These images were linked by Dr Travis to her frame-securing trigger and then to the patient's own frame-securing decision. Despite the intense pain of these fresh recollections and the activated existential and predatory death anxieties they revealed, a deep sense of accomplishment was reflected in the allusion to Grace's success as an artist. Ms Potter's failures in life and her dread of sudden death were also seen as self-punishments for real and/or imagined crimes against her sister, including her belief, which had some basis in reality, that she had contributed to her sister's death [the story of the woman who killed herself after killing her son].

Further discussion of the vignette

Several key points can be made based on this vignette:

1. The bilateral securing of the frame of this therapy had two dramatic effects on Ms Potter and the material she made available for trigger-decoding and eventual access to awareness.
   a. The securing of the frame enabled the patient to shift from a defensive enactment mode of coping to a controlled, imagistic communicative mode. The result was the emergence of meaningful and workable images related to her deeply unconscious experience of the death of her sister and the direct recall of aspects of her sister's death that had been subjected to strong conscious-system repression. The secured-frame moment lessened both conscious-system and deep-unconscious-system repression and the obliterating communicative defences of which they were a part. This response suggests that deviant frames interfere with the communication of encoded derivatives and with direct recall of repressed events, while the secured frame facilitates these processes.

b. The second effect of securing the ground rules of the therapy was the experience of secured-frame ego enhancement, followed by secured-frame anxieties related to unconscious feelings of entrapment and annihilation. These unconscious fears are connected to existential death anxieties in ways that are terrifying yet open to exploration and working through towards some measure of resolution. The excessive intensity of the death-related trauma and the patient's probable culpability are major factors in the predatory death anxieties that also emerged—an eye for an eye, a death for a death.

2. The potential to decode, recall, and work through death-related experiences appears to be rather different under each of three possible conditions:

   a. *When the frame is stabilized and there are no active frame issues and interventions.* At such times there is little deep unconscious activity. In this clinical example, the overall frame had been stable until the lecture was announced, although there was at least one background deviation—Dr Travis' publication of a magazine article that the patient had read.

   b. *When the frame is modified by the patient or therapist through a change in or violation of a ground rule.* This is the kind of event that is unconsciously experienced as a form of death-related persecution, accompanied by the activation of danger-situation, predatory death anxieties. At such times, the deep unconscious system will work over the deviation, but critical portions of the death-related deep unconscious perceptions and memories will not become accessible for trigger-decoding and working through. This occurs because they do not find encoded representation under these conditions in which the therapist is unconsciously experienced as highly dangerous and untrustworthy.

   c. *When an altered or insecure frame is actively secured.* Under these conditions, extensive existential secured-frame anxieties are activated and the patient will encode a wide range of previously unavailable, deeply repressed memories that are accessible to trigger-decoding. Supplemented by the direct recall of superficially repressed recollections, the experience is terrifying, but it is highly therapeutic if properly managed and interpreted.

3. Secured-frame moments are essential to any deeply insightful cure. They are the only means through which existential death anxieties are mobilized in a manner that is potentially therapeutic—that is, accessible to trigger-decoding and meaningful insight.
4. Survivors of death-related events virtually always experience survivor and other forms of guilt when a loved one dies. This guilt resides in the fear/guilt subsystem of the deep unconscious system and exerts powerful effects on conscious decisions and behaviours, often with little in the way of conscious insight or encoded representations that might make these issues available for trigger-decoding and working through. In this case, unconscious guilt was a major factor in Ms Potter's impoverished life; her guilt repeatedly unknowingly motivated her to make choices that were self-defeating and self-punitive. Secured-frame moments open the door to gaining workable access to these conflicts and unconscious forces, enabling them to be worked through and resolved.

Children also borrow survivor and other forms of guilt, along with extremely strong defences against death anxiety, from parents who have suffered significant death-related traumas—as seen with the children of concentration-camp survivors. The parents' death-related history is part of the child's history as well.

SOME FINAL PERSPECTIVES

I have argued that the complexities and depths of human reactions to death-related experiences are generally unappreciated. Much of the power of these events is processed by the deep unconscious system of the emotion-processing mind and is stored in its memory system. These meanings are accessible for resolution only via trigger-decoding. The superficial working-over of these issues in terms of manifest contents, their implications, and evident ties differs greatly from work with activated encoded contents related to the deep unconscious processing of these death-related experiences. These latter responses are, in general, expressed as disguised reactions to a therapist's frame-management interventions.

Frame-securing interventions in particular activate the deeply repressed meanings of a patient's most traumatic death-connected experiences. Nevertheless, it is only under frame-securing conditions that the triggers and decodable themes become available in workable form, allowing for significant reduction in the ill effects of these terrible traumas.

Finally, there is a great difference between the effects of non-decoded, uninterpreted, deeply repressed traumatic death-connected experiences and their meanings on the one hand, and the death anxieties aroused by secured frames and trigger-decoded images on the other. In the first situation the result is various forms of pathological defensiveness and maladaptation, while the second leads to deep insight and enhanced adaptation—both to death-related issues and in general. Such are some of the communicative insights into these difficult areas.

CHAPTER SIX

The emotion-processing mind

The communicative approach embraces adaptation and communication as its fundamentals. This strategy has led to the careful definition of conscious and unconscious communication as described in the chapter 5. Communicative listening and formulating made it possible to explore and map the architecture of the emotion-processing mind—the cognitive mental module that is responsible for adapting to emotionally charged impingements or triggering events. Definition of this module has made feasible a scenario for its evolutionary history and development and generated fresh insights into its immediate adaptive functioning.

The *emotion-processing mind* is composed of two systems—*the conscious system* and *the deep unconscious system*. Each system adapts in very different ways to death and death-related issues. It therefore behoves us to define the distinctive adaptive resources and strategies utilized by each system so we can appreciate the differences between conscious and unconscious coping efforts in these areas.

THE EMOTION-PROCESSING MIND

The emotion-processing mind is an evolved organ of adaptation with two parallel processing systems. One system is linked directly to awareness, and the other lacks such a link. Because of this arrangement, humans have two rather different ways of experiencing their *environments* (a comprehensive term that includes both living and non-living surroundings and impingements). This dichotomy of experience results in two views of emotional life. The first is manifest and largely within awareness, while the second is entirely outside direct awareness and is definable only through the trigger-decoding process.

The conscious and deep unconscious systems of the mind depend on intakes from the environment via *conscious and unconscious perception*, respectively. The mode of experience is determined by an emotionally charged *gating mechanism* that is influenced by *both the nature and emotional charge of the triggering event and the inner state of the perceiver.* This perceptive process is *personally selective* in terms of the consensually validated meanings of a particular event. Furthermore, registration in one form excludes registration and processing in the other. Each system creates its own distinctive version of reality. Events and communications from self and others do not enter the mind as simple, directly transmitted bits of information and meaning, nor is every potentially available impingement registered consciously or unconsciously.

The two systems of the emotion-processing mind have evolved structures that selectively perceive and accept meanings from those aspects of the environment that it has been internally configured to experience. By design, the conscious system is sensitive to a broad range of environmental impingements, but it is relatively insensitive to ground-rule- and frame-related events and their meanings. On the other hand, the deep unconscious system is exceedingly frame-sensitive and relatively impervious to most other kinds of external happenings and their meanings.

In humans, the *adaptive functioning* of each system is *language-based*—each relies on the single greatest resource to have evolved in *Homo sapiens sapiens*, the use of words and sentences to represent the world internally in order to deal with its impingements and to find novel and effective solutions to the problems they impose—and to communicate and develop shared or conjoint adaptive capabilities with others.

AN EVOLUTIONARY SCENARIO

An evolutionary perspective is helpful for understanding the current architecture and functioning of the two systems of the emotion-processing mind. Historically, with the advent of the hominid line, the conscious system developed first some 6 million years ago (Langs, 1996). It is the system that is responsible for immediate and long-term survival, and it draws on a wide range of cognitive and coping capacities, including efficient perception, audition, and other sensory intake channels; the ability to think, reason, and solve novel problems with unique solutions; the capacity to relate and communicate; and a means of rapid physical responsiveness, especially at times of physical danger.

The evolving hominids greatly expanded family and social commitments, and their social burdens grew enormously. Pressures also escalated as technologies became more complex and dangerous. The growing intricacies of emotional life led to a striking increase in personal emotional impingements and in the knowledge needed for the basic insurance of safety, shelter, energy, and reproductive success. These developments overloaded this fledgling conscious system to the point where personal and species survival were at issue.

Some 100,000 to 150,000 years ago, language capabilities developed, possibly as a means of coping better with the complexities of human interaction. Language acquisition enhanced human resourcefulness beyond that of any prior species, yet it also greatly intensified both the nature and the range of dangers faced by humans. Because of the use of language, death became a consciously articulated concept and one of the major dangers to emotional well-being. The death and loss of others, and threats of personal annihilation, were also specifically defined by this means, although language use also enhanced the capacity of humans to deal with these traumas.

Language was largely responsible for the development of clear self/not-self boundaries, and therefore it facilitated the development of a strong sense of personal identity, which led to the articulation of one's personal existence, which had, of course, both a beginning and an end. Language also contributed to our remarkable abilities to remember and mentally work over past events, and enabled us to anticipate the future definitively. This latter ability included all manner of death-related threats and experiences.

In response to many selection pressures, the cognitive mind evolved with a stress on increasingly effective and creative conscious coping resources that enhanced one's knowledge of the environment and its dangers—and with that, one's chances of survival. The evolution of these non-emotional, survival-related cognitive abilities stressed awareness of one's surroundings and of others with little in the way of mental defensiveness, although physical protective measures were at a premium. Rewarded and selected were increasingly clever means of self-protection and of finding shelter, food, and companionship.

As conscious-system overload began to endanger individuals, natural selection evidently favoured the relegation of emotional experiences and their increasingly complex meanings—including the existential awareness of death and aspects of a sharpened awareness of predatory threats—to unconscious perception, so they would no longer disrupt conscious-system efforts to satisfy basic needs for survival and safety. Because of the little available time by evolutionary standards that natural selection has had in which to effect these changes, nature appears to have mainly selected for minds that are exceedingly defensive psychologically and communicatively regarding the emotional aspects of human life.

The following considerations seem to have been pertinent to the selection of favourably adaptive emotion-processing minds:

1. Survival-adaptive capacities were afforded prime consideration and safeguarded at all cost.
2. Cognitive evolution relied to a large extent on language development and stressed both creative modes of adapting and astute forms of physical and mental defence.

3. Emotional impingements, including those related to death, were experienced largely as dangers to survival-related cognitive functioning.
4. Emotional needs were subjugated to more essential needs to survive.
5. The overload of pressures on the capacities of the single-system conscious mind caused natural selection to favour a two-system mind. When a system is overloaded with information and meaning, nature commonly tends to create a new system to handle the excess.
6. Natural selection chooses from random and self-organizing variations those that most favour survival and reproductive success vis-à-vis the prevailing environmental conditions and impingements. The process requires very long periods of time—hundreds of thousands to millions of years. Thus, the evolution of the language-based emotion-processing mind is in its infancy. As a result, compromises and trade-offs have been inevitable, and they have proven to be primarily obliterating and defensive in nature.
7. In order not to disrupt conscious-system functioning and adaptation, the second system had to operate outside awareness. This was accomplished in two ways:
    a. By relegating memories of once conscious events and meanings to a superficial unconscious storage system that is safeguarded by a defensive, repressive barrier. In this way, language-based memories that are too anxiety-provoking and thereby disruptive to conscious-system functioning are barred from awareness.
    b. By selecting for minds capable of unconscious perception and processing of potentially disorganizing emotional impingements and meanings of events that can be excluded from awareness without seriously endangering the immediate survival of the individual. This mechanism is a compromise in that it bypasses awareness and protects the conscious system but does so by *reducing the person's knowledge of the environment and some of its more dangerous aspects*—its use can prove costly in the long run.

These disturbing emotional meanings reach awareness only in encoded form. *Disguise and displacement* are the protective *psychological and communicative devices* selected as the means of encoding these meanings. And these devices are only moderately successful in reducing the anxiety level of the individual. The conscious mind is inherently antagonistic towards encoded imagery because of its threatening latent contents, and is even more antagonistic to efforts at trigger-decoding because they will reveal the raw nature of unconscious experiences.

8. The net result of nature's sequence of selections is a two-system mind that safeguards conscious-system survival efforts, but does so through a very expensive trade-off. The limitations of adaptive resourcefulness in the emotional domain is immense:
   a. There is a considerable amount of *knowledge reduction* with respect to the conscious awareness of emotional impingements, resulting in a great loss of sensitivity and self-protection.
   b. There is also an inherent dread in all humans of encoded communication and meanings that defeats most efforts at self-exploration and trigger-decoding—with considerable loss of useful deep insights. These anxieties also cause patients and prospective patients (and colleagues) to fear and oppose therapists who engage in trigger-decoding.
   c. The use of displacement leads to behaviour that is enacted with one person whereas it is primarily and unconsciously a reaction to another person. This leads to a wide range of interpersonal difficulties and emotional symptoms.
   d. The lack of a conscious awareness of the most powerful perceptions and meanings in emotional life leads to misdirected and destructive behaviours, affects, and responses.
9. The deep unconscious system has its own intelligence embodied in a *wisdom subsystem*—a set of ego functions comparable to, but differently constructed from, the conscious system's ego functions. The adaptive choices made by this deep system in response to emotionally related triggering events is far superior to that of the defensively motivated and perceptually blocked conscious system. The deep unconscious system focuses on the

most compelling meanings of an emotional experience. These pertain to its ground rule and frame implications—aspects minimized or entirely missed by the conscious system.

The survival value of this deep unconscious sensitivity lies with the importance of secured frames as a foundation for personal safety, growth, invention, and creativity. The finding that these sensitivities are deeply unconscious and that they reach awareness only in encoded form can be attributed to the intensity of the death-related secured-frame anxieties experience by all humans.

10. The evolution of the emotion-processing mind is overweighted towards defence at the expense of creativity.
11. In another complex development, mainly based on efforts to control conspecific violence and to handle the newly articulated awareness of death, natural selection has opted for two deep unconscious subsystems—*the aforementioned wisdom subsystem* (see Point 9 above) *and a fear–guilt subsystem*.

    The fear–guilt subsystem, which embodies guilt for real and imagined harm caused to self and others, along with the existential fear of death, has been designed so that it exerts a strong but unconscious influence on the conscious system. While the emotion-processing mind as currently configured cannot benefit from deep unconscious wisdom because of the strong defensive needs of the conscious system, it is affected by deep unconscious fear and guilt. These latter motivating systems play a major role in constraining acts of violence and harm, thereby favouring personal survival. Because the control of vengeful and self-serving violence is a prime issue among humans, this subsystem has therefore evolved with considerable unconscious influence in the emotional sphere.

THE CONSCIOUS SYSTEM

The conscious system has been fashioned with a very wide range of sensitivities, though it is programmed by natural selection to miss a great deal as well. It is the system that effects immediate adaptations and is therefore responsible for long- and short-term survival. The conscious mind is capable of receiving a vast view of its immediate environs, and it possesses a great capacity for both memory of the past and anticipation of the future.

The conscious system's perceptive scope is so wide that we seldom realize its limitations. Physiologically, they include insensitivity to parts of the spectra of light, to vast ranges of sound, and to many aspects of the environment to which other species are highly attuned. Psychologically, the system is focused on the surface meanings of emotionally charged events, and in thinking about these events it is naturally inclined to do so in terms of psychodynamic and personal genetic issues—sexual and aggressive needs and conflicts, psychic defences, and the like—and naive ideas about relating and relationships, self and identity.

All of this is so natural to us that we have had little sense of the restrictions and blind spots of the system in its experience of emotional life. But the conscious system's psychological adaptive concerns are built around but two of the ten hierarchies of psychoanalysis that define the enormous range of emotionally charged implications and meanings that accrue to an emotional experience or therapeutic interlude. The conscious system has little inclination or capacity to think in terms of systems, science, design of the mind, mind rather brain, and especially rules, frames, and boundaries. Each of these realms is a critical aspect of emotional life and adaptation.

Overall, because the need for mental defence was perhaps the major driving force or selection pressure in the evolution of its design, the conscious system is insensitive to many aspects of human emotional experiences with which the deep unconscious system is quite in touch. As I have begun to show, many of these unperceived meanings are related to trigger events that activate the problems of death and death anxiety.

THE DEEP UNCONSCIOUS SYSTEM

The evolved deep unconscious system of the emotion-processing mind experiences the emotional world almost exclusively in terms of rules, frames, and boundaries. Where the conscious system is broadly concerned but overlooks many frame-related events and meanings, the purview of the deep unconscious system is exceedingly narrow. While psychodynamic, interpersonal, and personal genetic factors play a role in the operations of this system, these aspects are aroused by and viewed in terms of activated frame issues that lie at the core of deep unconscious experience.

The deep unconscious system is activated by the frame aspects of the present moment and relationship, which includes carry-overs of frame issues stemming from recent interactions with the individual at hand. Because frame impingements tend to be perceived and registered unconsciously, perceptions and processing activities in response to this type of impingement reach awareness only in encoded form. Much of frame-related experience occurs without direct awareness, and its transformation into conscious experience requires trigger-decoding efforts.

Thus, in psychotherapy it is possible to work over and work through a patient's deep unconscious responses to death-related issues only when there is an active frame-connected triggering event—either frame-securing or frame-modifying—created by the therapist within the therapy. In the absence of such an event, the deep unconscious system is inactive and lies fallow. However, in the presence of such a trigger, all of the psychodynamic and personal genetic aspects of the stimulus and its connections to death emerge via encoded narratives, available for trigger-decoding—and for insight and the development of fresh and favourable adaptations.

A FINAL NOTE

Secured-frame anxieties related to existential death anxiety are largely responsible for the frame-related attitudes of the two systems of the emotion-processing mind. Frame modifications are favoured by the conscious system of the emotion-processing mind as a means of denying vulnerability to both forms of death—aggressive or predatory and existential or inevitable. Because of its ties to expressions of death anxiety, secured frames tend to be dreaded and avoided by the conscious mind. In contrast, the deep unconscious system does not have major secured-frame anxieties, and the system consistently encodes its preferences for secured frames. These preferences prove critical to the ways in which humans attempt to cope with death and its attendant anxieties. Death is a strong shaping force in the design of the emotion-processing mind.

CHAPTER SEVEN

Death and the two systems of the mind

As indicated in chapter 6, humans operate and adapt by means of two very different systems of the emotion-processing mind, one linked directly to awareness, the other connected only through encoded images and unseen effects. Each system has distinctive properties—selective areas of perception; processing capabilities; motivational tendencies and needs; resources, defences, and frame-related attitudes; ways of assessing, thinking and formulating; and overall adaptive capacities and inclinations. Not surprisingly, then, these two basic systems also differ in their experience and processing of death and its related impingements. These differences are best appreciated through an understanding of the evolutionary history of the awareness of death as a twofold danger situation—one existential and the other predatory in nature.

THE EVOLVED AWARENESS OF DEATH

An individual's ontogenic development of the awareness of death and of responsive adaptive resources to cope with death-related triggering events is grounded in phylogeny or evolutionary history. How, then, did awareness of death—predatory and existential—evolve, and what effects did this awareness have in shaping the design of the emotion-processing mind?

As I indicated in chapter 1, the predecessors to the hominid line, such as apes and other advanced mammals, show a global and at times incisive awareness of predatory danger. The extent to which this entails a realization of the specific danger of annihilation is uncertain, but there is evidence that serious threats to life evoke powerful adaptive responses. This sense of possible doom appears to have facilitated the development of defensive and other life-saving skills that thereby enhanced individual and species survival. These capabilities are a mixture of instinctive and learned resources, and they are bound to immediate situations and to relatively fixed avoidances or assaultive counteractions.

As for the existential form of death anxiety, there is evidence that apes and other mammals mourn their dead, as seen when a mother loses an offspring. Some animals show signs of an awareness that they are dying—for example, elephants leave their herds to die. But here too the "awareness" appears to be relatively automatic and instinctive; it does not lead to complex or flexible behaviours.

Language development was the pivotal evolutionary event that changed this entire scenario. By facilitating representation and communication, language enabled humans to develop definitive representations of self as distinct from others. Language allowed for the specific definition, retention, and mental working over of past events, the realization of vast amounts of death-related meaning in present interludes, and the elaborate anticipation of future possibilities. Predatory forms of death anxiety were made more explicit, and the existential form was precisely defined and became a vital aspect of human awareness.

Another consequence of language was the extension of predatory danger and threats of annihilation beyond physical perils into the psychological realm. Apes and some mammals experience psychological threat as part of certain physically based dangers, such as a young animal's response to the absence of a maternal figure. However, the range of definitive psychological life-endangering threat is far more extensive in *Homo sapiens sapiens* than in other species. These dangers are experienced on two levels—consciously and deeply unconsciously.

Hominids have evolved a capacity for both conscious and unconscious perceptions of death-related dangers, and they have developed adaptive resources on both levels. In addition, while apes show a sense of loss only after death has actually occurred, humans have an extensive capacity to anticipate death in themselves and in others. The perception of possible illness and impending death in others is a definitive experience in humans, operating also on both the conscious and deeply unconscious levels. In all, the range of potential causes for death anxiety of both the predatory and existential forms, and in reference to self and others—including the loss of others—is far greater for *Homo sapiens sapiens* than any other species.

In keeping with the nature of most organism–environmental-threat scenarios, as the awareness of the danger of death expanded, the resources available to the emotion-processing mind to cope with this danger were also augmented. However, this kind of "arms race" is seldom balanced equally on both sides, and often one side becomes more powerful than the other.

In this case, the spectre of death has generated far more trauma and disruption than the evolved resources of the emotion-processing mind is capable of coping with effectively. In particular, the development of a clearly represented self and the ability to foretell aspects of the future brought with them the specific, ever-present awareness of the inevitability of death of self and others: that is, existential death anxiety. Humans are especially vulnerable to this type of anxiety, and they have developed few means of dealing with it—forms of denial being the main mechanism (see chapter 11).

THE EFFECTS OF THE AWARENESS OF DEATH

Evolution unfolds through random variations that affect the capacity of organisms with given configurations to survive and reproduce in their immediate environments and the favourable reproduction of those behaviours and mental adaptations that are most successful in these endeavours. Self-organizing principles that are inherent to the development of single organisms and species may also play a role. Selection pressures in the environment operate to influence the results of these naturally selective processes. These principles apply to the awareness of death.

We are examining a relatively early historical scenario. Because the issues and responses are essentially language-based, natural selection has had very little evolutionary time—at most, some 150,000 years—to forge an effective survival-maximizing mental strategy for coping with death-related issues. To this date, then, the natural unfolding and development of the emotion-processing mind in light of the language-based awareness of death has had several kinds of unprecedented and powerful effects:

1. Awareness of both forms of death anxiety—predatory and existential—became a *selection pressure* that influenced the "mindless choices" made by natural selection. Selection pressures are, as a rule, environmental conditions and interactions that shape selective choices of organs and behaviours that favour survival.

   The actuality and awareness of death is, however, an unusual selection pressure. It has environmental, physical, and internal intrapsychic features. Thus, the danger of death may come from non-self-predators and involve a physical threat with emotional overtones; it may take the form of self-predation as seen in the impulse to commit suicide, a psychologically caused physical threat; it may come from the realization of the impending or actual death of others; and it may arise through the death of the body as existential death reaches its fulfilment.

   All told, the awareness of death as a selection pressure essentially is a unique combination of environmentally and internally derived forces. On the one hand, this awareness heightens one's sensitivity to external outer related dangers, leading to an enhanced sense of external threat and improved adaptive resources. But, on the other hand, the awareness itself is intrapsychic and it is thereby an internally configured, self-directed, self-made selection pressure of a type first written about by Baldwin (1896). In humans, then, emotionally charged selections pressures are located in both the environment and the self.

In addition to the role played by conscious awareness of death and death-related traumas, humans experience unconscious perceptions of these threats, especially when they are psychological in nature. However, every external endangerment is also fraught with psychological meaning, and many of the most threatening aspects of these experiences are perceived and processed outside awareness. They then exert their effects quite unconsciously, although their role as part of evolutionary selection pressures can be considerable.

In its many facets, aggression and violence, as perceived in others and self, consciously and unconsciously, and the annihilations and death anxieties that they create, are among the most powerful selection pressures and driving forces in emotional evolution for the hominid species and each of its individual members.

2. With respect to the early hominids, the overwhelmingly traumatic qualities of the conscious and unconscious experiences of death and death anxiety are likely to have caused system overload for the early single conscious-system emotion-processing mind. These disruptive and distracting impingements, especially as they pertained to death anxiety, were a key aspect of the selection pressures and threat to survival that led to the evolution of a second system for the emotion-processing mind—the deep unconscious system.

   By means of unconscious perception, many death-related traumas and meanings could be experienced and processed entirely without awareness interceding. The conscious system was freed of a great burden and source of disruptive anxiety, thereby allowing the system to operate more smoothly than otherwise.

3. The selected design of the emotion-processing mind was affected by the limited evolutionary time available for natural experimentation and choice and, most critically, by the unique

attributes of death as a danger situation and especially its ultimate inexorable power—its fateful existential triumph. As a result of these factors, natural selection has favoured the perpetuation of *highly defensive* emotion-processing minds to deal with death-related—and thereby all emotionally charged—adaptation-evoking impingements. Most favoured were the psychological defences of denial and repression, and the communicative defences of non-communnication and disguise. Basically, this means that many aspects of death-related experiences and memories tend to be expressed indirectly via displaced and disguised allusions or not expressed at all.

In sum, then, the desperate need to neutralize and cope with unrelenting existential death anxieties played a key role in the evolution of this mental module and especially in the stress on defensive formations in its historical unfolding over time.

The invocation of unconscious perception and obliterating communicative defences are unusual choices for natural selection, which is inclined to favour minds that enhance their capacities to experience the environment and communicate with others. Furthermore, language provided humans with a unique capacity to interact and communicate, yet death anxiety promoted the development of mental configurations and defences that led to the extensive use of language for non-communication in the service of survival.

4. Language also brought with it a strikingly definitive and disturbing awareness of death as a danger situation, and by doing so facilitated the development of new resources with which to combat the possibility of being annihilated or of dying from natural causes. With respect to predatory violence, from conspecifics and others, language facilitated the expansion of physical means of self-protection that could, through verbal communication, operate both individually and collectively through protective alliances.

   On the other hand, this same development led to an unprecedented elaboration of the available weaponry for murder and harm from conspecifics, rendering the threat of death especially strong. Social and psychological forms of harm and social inequities, as well as limitations of food and other resources, also expanded with language use. These developments intensified motivations to harm others to levels of intensity never before known. Destructive alliances, which are seen at times in apes, became a major threat to non-allied humans. Other forms of social destructiveness gained validity.

These observations suggest that *death anxiety may have been a crucial factor in the development of language* and in the evolutionary history of the hominid species. Language development appears to have been part of an arms race in which both the means of adapting to the danger of death and the causes of annihilation were enhanced. The present status of this struggle appears to favour harmful maladaptation over peaceful coping. In part this seems to stem from natural selection's inclination to favour defence formations rather than active coping skills, especially with respect to existential death anxieties. It remains to be seen whether recent shifts in human attitudes towards death and dying, which appear to be far more accepting and tolerant than before, will alter the balances between obliteration and active coping.

An important reason for the choice of defence over active coping is the language-realized fact that death is one of the few adaptation-evoking triggering events to which humans have no completely successful adaptive answer—death ensures that survival of the individual is ultimately not possible. Just as humans are helpless as infants in the hands of abusive parents and when subject to arbitrary authoritarian edicts, so nothing can be done adaptively to have full command over the issue of ultimate death. New skills may postpone the inevitable, but there are countless situations where no manner of present-day intelligence can prevent death from having its way on an individual basis.

Even on the species level, there are many global catastrophes with which the human mind and body are not—and may never be—able to cope. These disasters may be sudden events, like the planet being struck by an enormous meteor, or gradual, as may be happening at present through humans' own poisoning of their environment and the alarming eradication of both resources and other species needed for ecological balance.

5. Language has been a major factor in the role of aggression both in creating predatory death anxieties and in human adaptive and maladaptive responses to this issue. Well-defined conscious and unconscious death anxieties are a major unconscious motive for assaults on others—for aggressive behaviours of all kinds. These actions are one means through which death anxiety and helplessness are denied—they are *action forms of denial.*

   But here, too, the situation is complex. Aggressive impulses in others imply the danger of death, and language allows for both conscious and unconscious registration—and therefore for both knowing and unwitting adaptive responses. But aggression may be invoked as a means of personal survival—first, as part of an effort to ensure legitimate supplies of food, shelter, and the like, but, second, as a motivator to assault others in order to achieve these goals. Self-directed aggression may also at times be a constructive motivator or may lead to self-destruction.

   In all, aggression may cause death or be evocative of death anxiety on the one hand and, on the other, an adaptive or maladaptive means of coping with these same issues.

6. Aroused death anxiety has two contradictory effects on immediate adaptations.

   a. The first is a response to *predatory threats of violence.* This entails the mobilization of active, conscious-system functioning, the muting of unconscious perception and processing, and reliance on enhanced physical and mental skills of self-protection and counter-attack.

      Recent studies (Langs, 1996; Plotkin, 1994; see also Cziko, 1995) have shown that the choice of adaptive response to a particular predatory threat is primarily selected by the nature of the environmental danger as it activates innate and learned resources existing within the individual. The human mind operates as a *Darwin machine* (Calvin, 1991; Plotkin, 1994; see also Dawkins, 1983) and functions according to selectionistic principles (the environment selecting optimal responses from existing resources within the organism) rather than by blindly complying with instructions from the external world and its traumas (the environment creating the organism's responses, with little say from the organism). The mechanisms at work are similar to those found in the immune system—our front-line defence against microscopic predators, which operates so that the attacker selects its optimal agent of destruction from existing immunological resources (Burnet, 1959; Gazzaniga, 1992; Jerne, 1967). So, too, with the emotion-processing mind.

b. The second type of adaptation is mobilized by *existential death anxiety*, which is inherently overwhelming and immutable. In response to this type of danger, the adaptive alignment is almost the very opposite of the human response to predators. With existential death anxiety, the danger situation is sometimes manageable in the short run, but essentially unmanageable in the long term. As a result, the adaptive response favours active coping to deal with immediate threats of death that can be resolved over the short term (as with many illnesses and accidents). However, the more basic response is the mobilization of obliterating mental defences that are resourceful in preventing disruptive degrees of awareness of personal mortality. These defences are built around psychological and communicative and action forms of *denial*, the latter ranging from manic celebrations and mindless behaviours to murderous enactments.

The conflicting pressures that realizations related to death create lead to selection pressures that promote contradictory tendencies. In the name of enhanced survival, selection is called on to favour heightened awareness of threat on the one hand and inhibition of awareness on the other. This, too, is a rather unique situation. The same threat pressures the mind to evolve in mutually exclusive ways. While conflicting selection pressures are not uncommon in nature, this particular contradiction is exceedingly powerful and appears to be irresolvable—neither type of selection pressure can be eliminated or played down. Compromise was absolutely inevitable.

Among the crucial factors in the choice made by natural selection, a key role appears to have been played by the likely overload on the conscious system caused by an over-awareness of existential death and a hypersensitivity to predatory causes of death, especially in the emotional realm. Natural selection seems to have favoured shoring up the conscious system's abilities to deal with physical threats from predators and diminishing the system's preoccupation with the inevitability of death. This solution does not, however, seem fully satisfying: a basic design change was sorely needed.

In keeping with nature's inclination to create a new system when a first system is overloaded with information and meaning, the design change invoked to resolve this engineering problem was to select for two-system, parallel-processing emotion-processing minds and to divide the adaptive responsibilities between the systems—conscious and deeply unconscious. Indeed, it may be that the definitive awareness of future personal death was the primary selection pressure that led humans to develop their unique two-system minds.

Let us look closer now at how these two evolved systems experience and process death-related issues.

DEATH ISSUES AND THE CONSCIOUS SYSTEM

The conscious system—the conscious mind—is well aware of death. It deals with its actualization in the death of others and with the long-term inevitability of personal demise, and it is quite aware of the dire consequences of certain injuries and illnesses. All of these situations of actual or potential harm also have strong psychological meanings and emotional impact. *Indeed, the triggering events that touch upon death issues tend to have both physical and psychological components.*

Death is, then, a universal, consciously registered, pervasive danger situation that is unique among human threats. It is a background danger at all times, and at various points in a lifetime it becomes an acute danger as well. It is primarily a physical danger with psychological effects, but it may also involve extremes of psychological harm that constitute life-threatening impingements—as seen in the case of extremes of parental neglect and with abusive parents and spouses who drive their children and mates to suicide.

In general, the conscious system adapts by reducing one's awareness of death and its accoutrements. The system tends to bring these issues sharply into conscious focus only when they are activated by a specific triggering event. Conscious-system responses to these events involve both physical and mental measures. On the physical side, a wide range of self-protective and counter-attacking behavioural measures is available to the conscious system—anything from taking vitamins and having an annual physical examination to escaping from or killing a murderer.

Mental responses to death also vary, depending on the activating trigger event; they may be primarily adaptive or maladaptive. For example, predatory threats of death may activate reasonable levels of anxiety and fear or extremes of these affects, resulting in panic and paranoia. They may also cause realistic feelings of depression or a depressive psychosis, and they may evoke appropriate aggressive responsiveness or blind rage.

Subjective feelings include a realistic sense of vulnerability or utter helplessness, and plans for self-protection and reasonable vengeance or blind revenge—with accompanying sensible or extremes of guilt. Similarly, being subjected to predation may arouse reasonable or extremes of conflict and cause the activation of memories that are appropriately or inappropriately linked to the current event. The range of conscious-system responses is quite wide, and mixtures of healthy and neurotic reactions are not uncommon.

Conscious awareness of illness, injury, or death in others and in oneself arouses a similar variety of adaptive and maladaptive responses. Such realizations evoke a wide range of affects: feelings of loss and depression; some sense of vulnerability and helplessness; and memories and fantasies that often reflect considerable conflict and ambivalence towards the ill or dying person. The actual configuration of responsiveness depends both on the nature of the death-related issue and on the individual's death-related life history and coping capacities.

THE DEFENCES OF THE CONSCIOUS SYSTEM

The conscious mind is so attuned manifestly to acute death-related dangers and issues that the extent to which it responds defensively to these situations is difficult to appreciate. Nevertheless, there are two basic constellations of conscious-system defence that account for conscious responses to death-related triggering events: those that are inherent to the system's evolved architecture and those that are activated psychodynamically by a particular traumatic event.

1. *The immediate defences of the conscious system*

In general, conscious-system adaptive responses to a death-related situation are constricted, fairly self-evident, shallow, intellectualized, and relatively fixed and repetitive. If the response involves communicative defences such as obliteration, they are sustained virtually without change. If the reaction includes an action form of defence, such as flight from a death-connected scene, the use of actions will also persist.

Conscious coping reactions to a death situation that involve mentation tend to involve going over the same territory again and again. Working through is superficial, and it leads to very limited insights and little in the way of true resolution of the underlying issues and anxieties.

The primary psychological and communicative defences utilized by the conscious system are variants based on denial. Even when death is faced head on and there is an awareness of the affects and problems it activates, the conscious mind employs denial-based defences. This use of denial, when invoked within limits, is relatively adaptive in light of the inevitability and unresolvability of death.

While natural selection has yet to come up with another conscious-system form of protection, it has elaborated many forms of denial. These include non-communication, obliteration of thoughts, not registering a life-threatening physical problem, avoiding diagnostic physical procedures, manic celebrations, taking extreme risks, frame breaks, and sexual promiscuity. Because these defences are fundamentally obliterating in nature, they are difficult to recognize clinically—in patients and, even more, in therapists.

2. *Defensive design features of the emotion-processing mind*

By evolved design, the conscious system registers a limited number of highly filtered and selected meanings of a death-related event. The system does not record many pertinent implications of these provocative triggering events. The conscious system may also fail to register entire events linked to death. Furthermore, once a death-related event and some of its meanings have been perceived in awareness, later recall may be unfeasible—the conscious system often operates with an impenetrable superficial unconscious repressive defence.

The structure of this system also is such that consciously humans are generally unable to recognize the connection of non-death events to death issues unless the link is relatively transparent—for example, when loss and absence is involved in a triggering experience. The conscious dread of death and its linked experiences joins forces with the evolved design of the emotion-processing mind, itself a product of that dread, to render the conscious system highly insensitive to many aspects and nuances of death-related events.

The emotion-processing mind is equipped with gating or screening mechanisms that operate on the perceptual level to bypass conscious registration. The specific thresholds are based on the inherited structure of the emotion-processing mind and a given individual's personal life history, including death-related experiences—one's own and one's parents'. Psychodynamic factors of conflict and the like also play a role, as does a person's conscious and unconscious perceptions of others who are involved in the triggering event and an individual's adaptive resources, including his or her tolerance for consciously experienced death anxiety.

A vast amount of death-related information and meaning does not impact on the conscious mind, because it is automatically relegated to unconscious perception and processing in the deep unconscious system. As for the experiences and meanings that do reach awareness, the conscious system responds with relatively weak and fragile adaptive efforts. Humans may turn the experience of loss into a consciously orchestrated creative moment; but, more often than not, they tend to suffer a loss or other trauma, mourn and work through its effects to a limited extent, try not to let the event prompt self-destructive or otherwise irrational actions—and hope that time will heal the psychological wounds created by the traumatic experience and that death will fade into the background once again.

Conscious-system use of denial mechanisms, which may be invoked without awareness, reduces the potential disruptive consequences of death-connected events, but at the expense of the obliteration of significant meanings. It is impossible to adapt to unrecognized perceptions and meanings, and this limits the success of conscious-system coping efforts with regard to death-related triggers. In addition, the consciously obliterated meanings of such triggers remain unconsciously active—they are directed to deep unconscious experience and processing—and they detrimentally affect both psychological and physical states and behaviour.

As a result of this situation, therapists and patients tend defensively to favour limiting the exploration and working-through of a death-related triggering event to exploring conscious-system responses. The persistent, serious, harmful unconsciously driven negative behavioural and symptomatic consequences go unresolved. To change this outcome and prevent these detrimental consequences, it is essential to work with deep unconscious responses to these events—therein lies our most effective resource for dealing with these issues.

DEATH AND THE DEEP UNCONSCIOUS SYSTEM

Because of the extremely traumatic and often consciously unresolvable features of death-related experiences, many of the perceptions and processing of the multiple facets of these events are perceived, processed, and adapted to by the deep unconscious system of the emotion-processing mind in lieu of conscious-system registration and processing. In addition, a large measure of the processing of the non-death evocators of death anxiety—especially those that are well disguised, such as frame modifications—do not register in awareness and are directed to the deep unconscious system for appreciation and adaptation.

By design, virtually all of these processes and their outcomes are inaccessible to awareness in direct and adaptively useable form. They are, however, reflected in a patient's encoded narratives, are subject to trigger-decoding, and can by this means be transported into awareness and made available for dealing consciously with evoked death anxieties.

While the conscious system strives mightily to deny and shut out death-related thoughts, images, and events, the deep unconscious system, protected from conscious forms of awareness, faces death and its representations with few signs of avoidance or obliteration. The main exception to this forthrightness occurs at times of acute death-related danger and sudden loss. At these highly stressful moments, the deep unconscious system tends either to shut down and not generate derivatives (encoded narratives) or to create highly positive images that are structured as forms of *deep unconscious denial*.

For example, at such times a patient will offer tales of happy events, moments of power and success, and healthy individuals—the displaced narratives embrace cheerful and constructive themes in the face of a depressing moment of utter helplessness. The distinction between conscious-system and deep-unconscious-system denial is that the former defence is reflected in the absence of allusions to the death-related trigger, while the latter is seen in the invocation of uplifting encoded themes at times of dramatic loss and harm.

Except for these overwhelming moments in which deep unconscious defences appear to be mobilized, the deep unconscious system is highly perceptive and sensitive to the death-related meanings in all human experience. This includes an appreciation for non-evident death-related events such as modifying and securing ground rules—behaviours whose connections to death anxieties are almost never appreciated consciously (see chapter 13).

Unless it is dealing with a situation of immediate death-related shock, the deep unconscious system perceives and experiences the more dreadful meanings of death-connected events and processes them towards adaptive recommendations. The system recognizes the adverse symptomatic consequences of overly defensive reactions to death and related events and is able to appreciate and consider the personal genetic connections between these events and death-related past experiences. The encoded messages imparted by this system embody ways of dealing with these incidents more adaptively than is possible through inherently defensive conscious working over.

By bypassing consciousness, this working through is carried forth without overwhelming terror. Yet this same potential sense of panic accounts for the difficulties all parties have in engaging in the trigger-decoding process that will reveal these insightful operations. On the whole, humans experience a far greater dread of death-related experiences than hope for relief through deeply unconscious processed insights.

* * *

In addition to its wisdom subsystem, recall that the deep unconscious system also embodies a *fear–guilt subsystem* in which death plays a notable role. This subsystem is organized around the fear of death and activation of guilt in response to behaviours that are harmful to others and self. The processing carried out in this subsystem accounts for a large proportion of unconsciously driven, maladaptive human behaviour.

The two subsystems of the deep unconscious system of the emotion-processing mind—the wisdom and fear–guilt subsystems—have dramatically different effects on the conscious system and its coping efforts. The invaluable knowledge and adaptive resources of the deep unconscious wisdom system are *not* available for conscious adaptations and show few effects on conscious awareness—perhaps an occasional sense that something is amiss. On the other hand, the deep unconscious fear–guilt subsystem is a strong and compelling, though entirely unconscious, influence on conscious choices and behaviours. It is a major unseen source of emotional symptoms and harmful choices and actions.

This means that the unconscious fear of death, expressed through a deeply unconscious sense of total vulnerability, plays a critical role in the psychic economy and in determining adaptive and especially maladaptive conscious behaviours. On the maladaptive side, this subsystem unconsciously motivates essentially destructive actions designed unwittingly to deny this vulnerability and the insistent inevitability of personal death. Yet, on the adaptive side, the fear of death embodied in this subsystem operates to constrain natural inclinations to do violence to others and may also lead to remarkably creative thrusts—as seen in death-triggered literature, works of art, inventions, new discoveries, and the like.

Clinical evidence

Much of the evidence of the extent to which patients and their deep unconscious systems are preoccupied with working over death issues comes from experiences with what I call *empowered psychotherapy* situation (Langs, 1993). In this form of therapy, a patient is obliged to report a dream and to associate to its elements with narrative material as part of a 90-minute session. This narrative encoded imagery is followed by an intense search for triggers—an effort that is concentrated on the recent frame-related interventions of the therapist—and supplemented by a secondary search for the patient's own frame-related behaviours. The process culminates in the linking of the triggers to the encoded themes in the narrative material, and the result is the realization of definitive insights into the deep unconscious experience of these frame-relevant triggering events.

Experience with this therapy paradigm in which both encoded imagery and the search for critical adaptation-evoking triggers are maximized, has shown that regardless of the patient, virtually every session has notable death-related images in the pool of generated narrative themes. This suggests that some aspect of death and its unconscious sources and meanings are an ever-present preoccupation of patients' deep unconscious systems. Why is this so?

The answer lies with the therapist, the structure of the therapy, and the patient. The therapist and the structure of psychotherapy play their part because every frame-related intervention made by a therapist activates one or another form of death anxiety. Holding to the ideal ground rules and secured frame or modifying these basic tenets is a continual activity of every psychotherapist. This means that death-related encoded narratives are being activated by the therapist's frame-related efforts in virtually every session.

As a rule, secured frames evoke existential death anxieties (which may feel persecutory to patients who are vulnerable to death), while modified frames stir up predatory/persecutory forms. Thus, the implications of a patient's encoded death-related imagery will depend on the prevailing frame-related interventions of the therapist at any given point in time.

With frame-related activities as a constant adaptation-evoking stimulus, relegating a large portion of the perceptions and working-over of death issues to the deep unconscious system spares the conscious system a disruptive preoccupation with death and the resultant death anxieties. But, as noted, this protection is costly. There is considerable loss of conscious knowledge and understanding, and the stage is set for pathological forms of displacement, with resultant maladaptive actions and emotionally based dysfunctions. This is the rationale for rendering these unconscious processes conscious through trigger-decoding, so as to minimize or eliminate their detrimental effects.

A clinical case example

A case example shows how the communicative listening and formulating processes illuminate the death-related adaptive efforts of the two systems of the emotion-processing mind.

Mr Carson, a bachelor in his late twenties who tended to keep to himself and had problems relating to others, was in once-weekly empowered psychotherapy with Ms Park, a social worker. Early in his therapy, the patient began a session with a dream in which *he is away on vacation and learns that there has been a flood in the basement of his house.*

Before associating to the dream elements, Mr Carson brought up a request for a change in his session to a time that would be more convenient for him. He knew that Ms Park would not reply until he had completed his 40-minute exercise, which is the first component of this treatment paradigm. He simply hoped that they would be able to address the problem later in the session.

Mr Carson turned to *guided associating* [i.e. using the elements of the dream as a source of fresh narrative images—another feature of this form of therapy]. Being on vacation recalled an incident from his childhood which involved a violent quarrel between his parents. They had planned a trip for early July that year, but his father had changed his mind and rescheduled it. Then, when the new date was almost upon them, he changed their plans again. The patient's mother was furious, and he was confused. His father should have been consistent. His changing things around like that drove them to distraction.

Much later Mr Carson found out that his father, who was a contractor, had been under investigation for illegal kickbacks to suppliers—he could never say no to a crooked deal. The problem with the holiday had actually arisen because the father was under investigation as a result of a worker having been killed at the site of an office complex the father was building. The man who died was in a dangerous, forbidden area without a helmet and was struck by falling concrete. He was in the wrong place at the wrong time—he should not have been there.

Mr Carson could never rely on his father to keep his word on anything he promised to do. It was infuriating and must be one reason why he—Mr Carson—is so mistrustful of people. His father's erratic ways were a major reason Mr Carson left home in his early twenties. He has not spoken to his father since.

The communicative exploration of this material begins with the most probable relevant triggering event—the anticipation that the therapist would change the time of this patient's session. This kind of triggering event is termed an *imagined, anticipated trigger event,* so called because it has been proposed but not actually carried out and lies in the future. The importance of this category of triggers is that the deep unconscious system *will always process a proposed frame-securing or frame-modifying intervention, even if the conscious system simply makes the request and drops the subject.* This processing will centre on how the therapist will be perceived if he or she agrees to the patient's request—the deep unconscious system does not as a rule work over the possibility that the therapist will not accede to the request. Secondarily, the encoded themes will indicate the patient's perception of his or her own efforts to alter the ground rules of the therapy.

This imagery lends itself well to trigger-decoding. As is true in almost all cases, no sooner is the trigger announced and activated than the patient tells a narrative that encodes his unconscious perceptions of the therapist should she change the time of the session. In the excerpt, the story bridges over to (reveals its connection with) the triggering event through the theme of *changing a schedule. Bridging imagery* of this kind is an essential marker of an activated triggering event that the patient's deep unconscious system is working over and adapting to at a given moment.

Next, themes are extracted from the encoded story and linked to the triggering event. The encoded themes represent valid perceptions of and adaptive responses to the deeply unconscious meanings and implications of the potential frame change. In addition, we try to ascertain the encoded recommendations of the patient's deep unconscious wisdom subsystem as to how the situation should best be handled. The narratives typically contain encoded *correctives or models of rectification.*

Based on a sound reading of the patient's narrative material, the patient or therapist in empowered psychotherapy needs to make a trigger-decoded interpretation and frame-management response. In this way, he or she can gain access to the patient's deep unconscious wisdom and understand and deal with the situation accordingly.

In this case, Mr Carson, with help from Ms Park, would ideally develop the following intervention from this material: if the therapist were to change the time of Mr Carson's sessions (which he consciously wants), he would experience her (unconsciously) as being as unreliable and dishonest as his father—changing the time of the session is being portrayed as being erratic like his father and as a corrupt deal of the kind his father would make (the personal genetic connection to the anticipated frame change). The deviation would be seen as a broken promise (the promise of a secured frame and of a given time for the sessions—consistency is expected and speaks for a reliable therapist) and evoke great rage in Mr Carson. The change in time would also be experienced as allowing the patient into the therapist's office at an inappropriate time and make the therapeutic space very dangerous—a place where the patient would be endangered and seriously harmed or even killed (the death-related story of the construction worker).

The correct thing to do, according to Mr Carson's encoded stories, is to be consistent and not to change the scheduled times of the sessions, placing him in the wrong place at the wrong time. Were Ms Park not to adhere to this unconsciously stated advisory, Mr Carson would be so furious and feel so endangered that he might leave the treatment (leaving home and not speaking to his father).

* * *

This example of trigger-decoding illustrates the kinds of deep insights and frame-management responses that are unavailable through any other means. Decoding sequences of this kind also shows how the conscious system seeks frame modifications at the very same time that the deep unconscious system seeks secured frames—this is a basic split in the emotion-processing mind.

The death image is best interpreted to represent the frame modification as a harmful, predatory action. The image illustrates the patient's death-related, valid unconscious perceptions of frame breaks as a form of violence to the patient—and the therapist as well. The trigger-decoded interpretation of this image would bring the patient fresh insight into the immediate situation, support a frame-sustaining intervention by the therapist, and call forth extremely painful previously absent deep unconscious images.

> In this session, once the above-formulated intervention was pieced together by patient and therapist, Mr Carson laughed and said the last thing he wanted was for Ms Park to behave like his father—the time of the sessions should stay as is. Ms Park fully agreed.
>
> Mr Carson then said that it was a pain in the neck to have to be at his sessions at this time, but it all made sense. He supposed he should go back now to his dream for a new story [a fresh guided association]. The flooded basement brought to mind an incident from his childhood. He lived in a neighbourhood with three apartment houses, all owned by the same landlord and cared for by the same superintendent. The super, as he was called, was a friendly man who would play games with the children in the area, and he was well liked. He was also an excellent repairman; there was almost nothing he could not fix. But one day he was in the basement of one of the buildings when a boiler exploded, and he and one of the tenants were trapped and killed when a ceiling collapsed. The whole neighbourhood had gone into mourning.

This is fresh narrative material with a new death image. We therefore need to ascertain the triggering event that has evoked these themes, so we can trigger-decode their activated meanings by linking the trigger to the themes. In trigger-decoding, themes need triggers, and triggers need themes. What, then, is the key trigger for this death-centred narrative?

The search for triggers is always pursued in the territory that the deep unconscious system works over—the immediate therapeutic interaction and the ground-rule-related interventions of the therapist (and secondarily of the patient). Here, the most immediate and cogent triggering event is Ms Park's indication that she would not be changing the time of Mr Carson's sessions—and, secondarily, the patient's consent to this decision.

This is a striking *frame-sustaining intervention and secured-frame moment* for both patient and therapist. That is, the therapist has, in the face of pressure to modify the ground rules of this therapy, elected to maintain and adhere to these rules—to keep the times as originally agreed upon. The patient's *conscious* response was one of slight annoyance and weak agreement with the decision—nothing more.

Let us now look at the response of his *deep unconscious system*, which, as his narrative indicates, is far richer and more meaningful than the constricted conscious reaction. To trigger-decode and formulate this imagery, we may note that at first there is a sequence of positive themes that reflect a favourable unconscious perception of the therapist in light of her frame-securing intervention. Unconsciously, she is seen as friendly and very effective and skilful, and she is well liked for what she has done. But there then follow the themes of entrapment and death. How are these themes to be understood?

The answer lies with the deep unconscious experience of a secured frame. This frame is experienced much the way life itself is experienced—as a great gift, but one that must end in death. That is, as noted, the securing of the frame activates existential death anxieties even as it offers deep support and comfort. These anxieties are configured around the entrapping qualities of a secured frame—the consistency is a source of trust and strength that nevertheless has enveloping qualities—for example, by confining the patient to a certain time and place for his sessions.

Notice that consciously there was no experience of support or entrapment, and certainly no sense of danger and death. These attributes of the intervention were experienced quite unconsciously and worked over in the deep unconscious system alone. Were these secured-frame anxieties to go uninterpreted, the patient might well act out—directly or via displacement—his need to flee the entrapment. For example, he might break his engagement to a woman well suited for him or quit his job because his boss was a stickler about work hours. Or he could go on a drinking binge to deny his activated death anxieties manically and cause himself considerable harm. Interpreting and working through secured-frame anxieties is one of the most therapeutic experiences a patient in psychotherapy can have—it greatly enhances his or her adaptations to death and its related issues.

SUMMING UP

In psychotherapy, then, death anxiety is not a single entity with a single type of cause or a single kind of meaning. There are deviant-frame death anxieties evoked by the actual predatory and psychologically annihilatory aspects of all frame modifications—a point illustrated here and in several earlier vignettes. But there are also secured-frame death anxieties in which support is experienced along with the inevitability of death.

Both types of frame-management events and death anxiety are pervasive in everyday life, much as they are in all psychotherapies. As practised today, however, frame modifications are far more frequent than are frame-securing interludes—as is true of all humans, the minds of therapists have evolved with conscious frame-modifying tendencies that are far stronger than those that are frame-securing. But as long as the triggers for the death imagery are properly identified, each type of interlude—secured or altered—can be the basis for effective therapeutic work and healing.

It is the responsibility of a therapist to ensure that this opportunity for insight and inner change is afforded to the patient. A therapist need not despair if one of his or her interventions has modified the frame—though hurtful for the moment, it is also a therapeutic opportunity in that, based on the patient's responsive material, both interpretation and rectification can be made, and much that is constructive can be achieved.

To turn this around, all frame-related interventions arouse one or another form of death anxiety. Because frame-management activities are ever-present in psychotherapy, death-related themes are also ever-present. They will be more than evident when a treatment situation is constructed in a manner that, as is true of empowered psychotherapy, allows for their full expression; they are more difficult to see in therapies that restrict the narrative communications from their patients.

* * *

We come back again to the defences that the emotion-processing mind possesses against realizations related to death. It is these defences that make death so difficult to explore and interpret and frames so difficult to manage. To clarify this issue, let us turn now to the therapeutic interaction to explore how patients and therapists deal with the critical issue of death anxiety from session to session.

PART TWO

DEATH ISSUES AND THE PATIENT

CHAPTER EIGHT

Death anxiety and the psychotherapy patient

I have endeavoured to broaden our perspectives on death-related issues and death anxiety as basic concerns of all humans. In this second part of the book, I concentrate on the therapeutic interaction and on how death anxieties evoke adaptations by both patients and therapists in the course of a treatment experience.

Death concerns are a universal problem for every human. Each person adapts to these issues on the basis of individual propensities activated by specific death-related triggering events. In the therapy situation, however, *the roles specifically assigned* to the patient and therapist define and constrain the means by which death issues are, in general, activated, expressed, and responded to—and, especially, how they can be resolved. While some overlap exists between patients and therapists regarding aspects of this problem, there are significant differences as well.

Three major interrelated facets of death anxiety play a role in psychotherapy:

1. *The triggering event*

Several types of triggers, distinguished for the most part by degrees of evident connection to death, activate these issues in psychotherapy. When approached through the communicative vantage-point, the psychotherapeutic situation affords a unique opportunity to study these triggers and the manner of response and evolved adaptation. The conscious and deep unconscious systems tend to be responsive to different death-related triggers and to different aspects of these triggering events. Here, we focus on patients' responses.

The activation of a death-related triggering event may involve incidents and actions that are manifestly connected with death, such as illness, injury, loss, and death itself. Or it may entail an action, planned or carried out, that latently and unconsciously is linked with death issues. In this regard, as I have tried to show, the most common class of events involves the framework and ground rules of therapy and whether they are secured or modified. On occasion, a frame-related experience in everyday life may activate a patient's death anxieties, and they subsequently find their way, through displacement, into the treatment experience.

A death-related triggering event may involve the patient personally or take place in his or her daily life, or it may arise from the therapist, either through a communication that directly involves illness, injury, or death or in the form of an indirect death-related intervention, such as a frame-securing or frame-modifying action.

While in principle therapists should not violate the ground rules of therapy through self-revelations, they may become ill and need to cancel one or more sessions (the reason for the cancellation should not be specified to the patient, but some therapists do so nonetheless). A therapist also may be injured in a way that is directly observable or have a lapse and reveal a personal illness or a death-related family crisis. In addition, a patient may accidentally obtain death-related information involving a therapist's personal life through a third party.

In general, manifest death-connected events in everyday life activate responses by patients' conscious systems to the surface meanings of the event, leading to conscious efforts at adaptation. In these instances, the deep unconscious system, which is, for the therapy patient, concentrated on the triggers created by the therapist, tends to be relatively inactive. Thus, the material in the sessions tends to be restricted to reflections of surface explorations and reactions, with little or no encoded imagery.

In principle, the deep unconscious aspects of death-related experiences are specifically activated by triggering events within the therapeutic interaction, without which they generally are not available for exploration, interpretation, and resolution. As noted, the most common death-related activating triggering event of this kind is a frame-related intervention by the therapist—most often, in today's practice, a frame modification. However, the patient may also be the activator of this type of death anxiety, as when he or she asks for a frame modification. In these instances, there is likely to be a prior frame-related intervention from the therapist that has served as the evocator of, and model for, the patient's frame-deviant request.

2. *The form of death anxiety—existential or predatory*

The nature of the activating triggering event determines the form of death anxiety that is aroused. Manifestly, harmful incidents arouse predatory death anxieties, whereas commitments evoke the existential form. Events in everyday life may arouse these anxieties, but the patient's tendency to work them over in therapy is minimal unless the outside event is linked to a comparable incident within the treatment situation.

Within therapy, incidents like illness and injury that involve a manifestly death-related event connected with the therapist will arouse predatory death anxieties in the patient. The source of these anxieties is twofold: (1) the harm to the therapist is always experienced in predatory terms, even when illness is involved; (2) the revelation of the problem is a frame modification that alters the relative anonymity of the therapist and thereby evokes traumatic forms of death anxiety.

In contrast, frame-securing interventions hold the patient well, and they have commitment, safety, and health-giving attributes; unconsciously, however, they activate strong and morbid forms of existential death anxiety. For highly traumatized patients, especially those who have suffered intensely disturbing death and death-related experiences, these secured-frame anxieties may seem persecutory because of their intensity. In all instances, however, for both patient and therapist, secured-frame anxieties are far more terrifying unconsciously than are the anxieties evoked by modified frames. Were it not for the unmatched and vital healing qualities of secured frames, the fundamental anxieties they evoke would render secured-frame therapies even more infrequent than they are at present.

3. *The response to the death-related stimulus or trigger*

A patient's response to a death-related triggering event may be essentially adaptive or maladaptive. The assessment of the nature of the reaction must take into account both conscious and unconscious experience. Thus, the therapist must attend to death anxieties that are aroused by events that are manifestly linked to death, and those, like frame-related events, that are latently connected.

On the adaptive side, the patient evidences positive coping responses that reflect effective emotional adaptive capacities. There is no evidence of actions that cause harm to self or others, and there may be creative activities. In addition, there is no threat posed to the continuation of the therapy and no efforts by the patient to modify the frame, and the defences used by the patient do not result in dysfunction or communicative blocking. Instead, encoded narrative material is available for the interpretation of the patient's deeply unconscious responses to the death-related trigger.

On the maladaptive side, there is activation of defensive responses, which leads to dysfunctional behaviours and disturbances in the therapy situation and in the patient's efforts to express himself or herself in a meaningful, interpretable manner.

The specific defences used by the patient are, as we have seen, a net result of the inherited architecture of the emotion-processing mind, the developmental experiences of the individual, and the psychodynamics of the triggering situation. Because death anxiety plays such a pivotal role in the defensive alignment of patients, the investigation of the defences created by and used to adapt to death anxiety enables us to clarify the nature of human mental defences as adaptive devices in general.

In an actual therapeutic experience, the patient's manifestations of death anxiety and his or her ways of coping and defending against these anxieties are features of *the patient/therapist system*. They are continually influenced by the therapist's interventions and the spiralling of the unfolding therapeutic interaction. Furthermore, the therapist's interventions—especially those that pertain to the ground rules of the therapy—are the primary triggering events that arouse the patient's deep unconscious death anxieties and other unconscious issues concerning the experience of death.

DECIDING FOR THERAPY

From the first thought of seeking therapy, a potential patient's death-related history, sensitivities, and issues affect the choice of a psychotherapist and treatment modality in many ways. In choosing a therapist, conscious considerations—such as the likely fee, the availability of a therapist, preferences regarding the professional degree and training, recommendations of others—are greatly influenced by deep unconscious needs. This is a typical example of how conscious reasoning and choices are driven by deeply unconscious motives and needs.

The key deep unconscious issues regarding the selection of a therapist and treatment modality pertain (1) to the extent to which a therapist is expected to *pursue unconscious meaning* of any kind, and *deep unconscious meaning* in particular, and (2) to the *status of the framework of the therapy*—whether it is or will be essentially modified or likely to be secured.

The patient's advance knowledge about the therapist plays a notable role in this selection process. Beyond consciously known attributes, the implications of this information are unconsciously perceived and processed with exquisite precision.

In this regard, three issues are basic and pertinent:

1. *The severity of the patient's death-related life history.*
2. *The nature of his or her currently active death-related issues, including recent relevant traumas.*
3. *The status of the patient's defences against death anxiety.*

In general, the more severe a patient's death-related life experiences, the more active recent traumas, and the more fragile his or her defences against death anxieties, the more likely it will be that a patient will seek a treatment form that is cognitive, surface-oriented, and frame-modified. Although exceptions do occur, by and large these traumatized individuals do not seek therapists who are likely to permit extensive narrative communication without interrupting and shifting over to the intellectualizing mode.

These patients look for therapists who are not going to allow deep unconscious meaning to be expressed and who are inclined to frame-modified treatment situations. Their preferences typically included clinic- and insurance-covered treatment situations, referrals by friends who are seeing or have been seen by a given therapist, therapists with whom there has been or presently is outside contact socially or professionally, and group therapy situations in which a secured frame is inherently impossible (the deviant presence of third parties to each patient's therapy is part of the definition of this therapy form).

Usually the choice of therapist begins with a prospective patient's selection of a referring individual or with the decision to seek treatment on his or her own. The nature of the referral source often influences the nature of the frame of the prospective therapy. In general, the ideal secured-frame referral would come from a medical doctor or some other knowledgeable professional who does not have a social relationship with the patient. The referral would be made with a recommendation based on professional capabilities, perhaps with a minimal statement of the therapist's qualifications and training. However, no personal information about the therapist would be revealed to the prospective patient, and the chosen therapist would not be personally known to the patient, nor would anyone the patient knows be involved with the therapist, professionally or otherwise.

Departures from this ideal are extremely common and reflect patients' general wish for frame-deviant treatment forms. This quest is unconsciously motivated by death anxieties residing in the highly influential fear–guilt subsystem of the deep unconscious system—the deep unconscious subsystem with the greatest unconscious effects on choices of this kind. Both existential and predatory forms of unresolved death anxiety propel patients unwittingly to seek maladaptive relief through frame-modified therapy contacts.

For example, a patient with an unresolved death issue caused by the recent death of a relative may accept a referral from another relative or see a therapist who is treating other family members. Unconsciously, this selection is made as a way of denying the recent loss and allaying the patient's death anxieties—the presence of others in the therapy situation serves as protection against total loss.

The selection of a deviant frame for the therapy will arouse predatory death anxieties. However, the maladaptive but handy defences against death anxiety offered by frame-modified therapies make this treatment form very appealing to patients. A deviant frame will reduce the patient's communication of encoded narratives and render the underlying death issues relatively unavailable for interpretation and working through. In addition, this type of coping effort leads to the patient's use of frame-deviant measures in his or her daily life—an action-discharge response that is costly to all concerned.

By way of contrast, a therapy that begins with a secured frame and with a therapist who is able to sustain it inherently evokes secured-frame existential anxieties. Nevertheless, these anxieties generally prompt the patient to communicate rich encoded narrative material, which is interpretable towards invaluable insight and improved adaptation. To do this, the patient must be able to tolerate his or her existential death anxieties until insight renders them non-disruptive. Secured frames are most conducive to the resolution of both forms of death anxiety.

Almost without exception, unresolved death anxiety is a significant motive for seeking therapy. This factor may be consciously experienced because of a known death-related event. But in many instances the presence and effects of death anxiety in prompting the search for a therapist are mediated unconsciously and go entirely unrecognized by the patient. The patient shows no inkling of the connection between a critical death-related experience and the decision for therapy. Very different conscious reasons are offered for this move, and these conscious reasons are often accepted at face value by the therapist as well—and so the underlying death issues go unrecognized and unresolved. Many stalemated therapies and so-called negative therapeutic reactions can be attributed to the failure to recognize latent death anxieties and issues.

SOME ISSUES IN TECHNIQUE

A patient will convey a great deal about these death-related issues in the telephone call made to arrange for a consultation with the therapist. It is critical for the therapist to inquire as to who referred the patient and to consider any possible prior contact with the caller. The patient will almost always reveal the existence of a basic frame alteration of this kind, and the therapist must intervene—"manage the frame"—at that very moment.

For example, a patient may identify another patient or a relative of the therapist as the referring source, or may allude to having met the therapist at a dinner party. The discovery of a major frame modification of this kind requires that the therapist not see the patient in therapy or even for a consultation session. In principle, it is best under these circumstances not to refer the patient to another therapist because the existing frame modification will contaminate the other therapy.

Essentially, the therapist should simply indicate that it is not possible to see the patient in therapy and suggest that the patient seek treatment with someone else. To say more risks further frame alterations. In particular, a refusal of a referral from another patient should not allude to the other patient—to do so violates the privacy and confidentiality of the other patient and is harmful to all three parties involved. It is important to be on the alert for these frame deviations because a large number of these telephone calls involve the patient's attempt unwittingly to involve the therapist in a misalliance designed to defend against active forms of death anxiety frame-deviantly and maladaptively. The therapist who secures the frame under these conditions offers a healing experience to the patient even though the patient is never seen in therapy.

If these defensive and pathologically satisfying deviations are not revealed by the patient or are missed by the therapist during the initial telephone call, this information is likely to be communicated again in the consultation session—the first session of the therapy. The frame deviation should be understood as a critical sign of maladaptation or acting out—an important patient-indicator or sign of pathology that has been motivated by unresolved death anxieties.

The therapist's participation in the deviation must also be recognized (it often is motivated by his or her own unresolved death anxieties—see chapter 15). This involvement becomes the main triggering event for the patient's deep unconscious system as reflected in the encoded narrative material. The therapist should listen for and organize the encoded themes around the frame-deviant trigger, which will make it possible to trigger-decode and interpret the patient's unconscious perceptions of the therapist's decision to see the patient under frame-modified conditions.

Almost always, the patient unconsciously perceives some type of death anxiety within the therapist as an unconscious motivating factor in such a frame-deviant decision. The therapist's interpretation should include this *realization as experienced and conveyed in encoded form by the patient* (and not as a confession or self-revelation by the therapist). The interpretation can then allude to the patient's own death anxieties and show how they played a role in the search for a frame-modified therapy.

Finally, the encoded material will direct the therapist's efforts at rectification. In most cases, discontinuation of the therapy is called for. If the patient continues in treatment, this constellation will keep reappearing and can be interpreted accordingly. In such cases, it is critical that the therapist keep the frame secured in all other respects so that the patient will have a basically frame-secured treatment experience after the initial frame break.

An important underlying factor in these deviant choices of therapist arises because unconsciously most if not all humans are despairing of successfully coping directly and in healthy ways with death and its attendant anxieties. As a result, potential patients (and their therapists) tend consciously to turn to maladaptive ways of dealing with these issues. This leads many patients to select maladaptively defensive frame-deviant therapy situations for their efforts at gaining emotional relief, despite the harm these choices may cause.

Frame modifications are ways of denying death and loss through maladaptive forms of merger, denial of separateness, blurring of boundaries, and by being the *exception to rules*—by implication, to the existential rule that death follows life. This is a major reason why frame-deviant forms of psychotherapy are so much in demand and practised so enthusiastically by most psychotherapists—the death-related issues that underlie this propensity are immense.

This also clarifies why the more severe the unresolved death anxieties, the more intense the search for—and the greater the likelihood that the prospective patient would seek out and accept—a frame-deviant therapist. Frame-securing interventions in the first session will activate overly intense death anxieties in these patients, who often flee the therapy rather than risk the terrors of a secured frame. They do so even though their encoded images validate the frame-securing and interpretative efforts of the therapist.

Carefully stated interpretations of these anxieties are at present the only available means of enabling these secured-frame-sensitive patients to stay in secured or re-secured forms of psychotherapy. Decoded unconscious meaning and understanding are sorely needed by these patients to enable them to resolve their severe death-related conflicts insightfully, but the meanings involved are greatly feared.

Secured-frame-sensitive patients create trying therapeutic situations for both patient and therapist. They call for a well-orchestrated, balanced approach with measures of frame-securing and deep interpretation in keeping with what the patient can tolerate. The therapist should be consistent and avoid both further frame alterations and shifts back and forth from frame-securing to frame-modifying interventions. Behaviours of this kind will very probably lead the patient to terminate the therapy. On the other hand, a consistent frame-securing and interpretative approach has the greatest chance of succeeding. The therapeutic problems created by death anxiety are plentiful and often difficult to negotiate.

CHAPTER NINE

How patients deal with death-related triggers

In ongoing psychotherapy, a patient's death anxiety is often signalled by the appearance of death-related themes, coupled with a variety of defensive responses. These compromised communications simultaneously reveal and conceal the unconscious death issues activated by a particular triggering event. And when the trigger involves a death-related trauma in the life of the therapist of which the patient is aware, the defences unconsciously mobilized by the patient may be all but intractable. The following vignette is illustrative:

> Ms Banks was in once-weekly empowered psychotherapy with Dr Tyler, a woman psychiatrist. The patient, who was in her late thirties, suffered from episodes of severe anxiety and a chronic sense of insecurity.
>
> Dr Tyler's teenage daughter had fallen ill with a serious form of bone cancer. On the Sunday before the session we will consider, the pastor of Dr Tyler's church had referred to the illness and had beseeched the congregation to pray for the young woman. Dr Tyler was at the hospital with her daughter, who

needed some special tests, so she was not present at the service. However, her patient, Ms Banks, had close friends in the neighbourhood and on occasion attended these services. At the beginning of this session Dr Tyler knew of the announcement, but she had no idea whether her patient had been in church that Sunday morning.

Ms Banks began the session by commenting that the therapist looked tired; she hoped she was well. She then reported a dream in *which she was in church with a strange-looking blonde woman. The pastor was giving a sermon on religion and health, but he looked odd because he had a cast on his leg and was on crutches.*

The main guided associations to the dream elements centred on two stories. The first involved an incident at Ms Banks' church one Sunday morning, when a woman had physically attacked the pastor, with whom she had evidently had an adulterous affair—a fact she announced to the congregation before going after him. When the pastor tried to get away from the woman, he fell and fractured his hip. He then suffered a long convalescence, which left him with a limp.

The blonde woman brought to mind a friend, Nan, who is blonde. She had recently developed cancer of the uterus and needed a hysterectomy. Ms Banks was concerned about her prognosis. She had gone to church with Nan and a group of her friends to pray for her recovery and cure. Nan had asked the people who came to church to keep her cancer secret from their other friends; she was afraid she might lose her job if word got around that she was ill. Nan had a friend who had developed breast cancer and had actually lost her job for a frivolous reason; the friend had died lonely and impoverished.

In the remaining time, during which Ms Banks attempted on her own to process her dream and discover the key triggers for her narrative imagery, she never once alluded either to being in church that past Sunday or to any knowledge of Dr Tyler's daughter's illness.

At this point in the session, then, Dr Tyler had no way of knowing whether the patient had experienced this trigger and was defending against its revelation or whether the patient had simply not heard the announcement. Had Ms Banks been present at the church service, the experience of the pastor's remarks would be considered a frame-deviant, *third-party self-revelation* triggering event. The pastor's announcement would modify the relative anonymity of the therapist by revealing personal information to the patient about a member of the therapist's family. Even when the therapist plays no role in a disclosure by a third party, the event is unconsciously experienced by the patient as the responsibility of the therapist—and therefore as a frame-breaking triggering event.

In light of clinical experience with defensive responses to frame modifications, the therapist should resist inner pressures to resolve the uncertainty with which she is faced by asking the patient some pertinent questions. She should adhere as much as possible to the ideal frame or ground rules of the therapy and allow the session to unfold on the patient's terms. In this instance, this means that the therapist should not further modify her relative anonymity by alluding to or providing hints about the church she attends or the illness of her daughter. No matter how suggestive the encoded images might be, it is possible that they stem from a triggering event other than the announced illness.

Were the therapist to make these disclosures to the patient, the intervention would be experienced as a devastatingly assaultive self-revelation. Even if the patient had indeed attended the service, the therapist's imposition would still constitute an attack on the patient's psychological repression/denial and communicatively obliterating defences. Doing so would create a premature confrontation with this frame-breaking event that would lead (1) to a sterile intellectual working-over of the trigger and (2) to a focus of the patient's deep unconscious system's activities on the therapist's need to assault the patient's defences and to modify the frame by revealing personal information—by means of this distraction from the therapist, the original deviant event would become a lesser issue. The two deviations also would compound the difficulties in understanding the effects of either one and the unconscious meanings of the original frame break would be especially obscured.

If Ms Banks had not been in church and did not know about Dr Tyler's daughter, this self-revealing frame break would be even more devastating for the patient. It would be experienced unconsciously as an uninvited frame-modifying intervention of considerable power. In either condition, the patient would perceive unconsciously and with validity that the self-disclosure was unconsciously motivated by the therapist's own unresolved death anxieties and by unconscious needs to distract the patient from her daughter's serious illness.

In principle, then, therapists should respect their patients' psychological and communicative trigger-evoked defences until the patients themselves modify their own obliterating response—or generate material that the therapist can trigger-decode in a way that sufficiently loosens these defences. Thus, in this case, Dr Tyler would work more effectively with her patient by following standard principles of technique in the hope of facilitating Ms Banks' resolution of her own meaning-eradicating defences—if they are, in fact, active at the moment.

In this regard, there is a considerable likelihood that the trigger is indeed known to the patient because of the closeness of these derivatives—that is, the use of themes that are strongly analogous or similar to those pertaining to the deviant trigger, themes that clearly bridge to and might readily represent the triggering event in question. This would imply that her defences have indeed taken command of her communications and her endeavours to carry forward and complete her responsive understanding and restitution efforts—her adaptive responses to the triggering event. Regardless of the prevailing trigger, the therapist must accept these defences until she and the patient find the means of enabling the patient to modify them.

EMPOWERED PSYCHOTHERAPY

Before returning to the session, to enable us to understand the nature of psychological and communicative defences better, a few words are in order regarding empowered psychotherapy:

1. It is a form of therapy that extends the communicative approach by creating a framework for the maximal communication of

encoded narratives and for an intense and active search for triggers.

2. Where the usual therapy forms allow the patient to free-associate and to sustain defences for long periods of time, empowered psychotherapy is inherently structured to challenge these defences and to expedite their resolution. It is therefore a method that optimizes deep unconscious expression and trigger-decoding.

3. It is a unique means of clinically *defining an optimal, non-defensive communicative process*—a standard against which the activities of both psychological and communicative defences can be gauged.

4. It is the treatment modality in which death-related themes appear with the greatest frequency and intensity, thereby fostering the understanding and working-through of these issues. While the principles of trigger-decoding apply to all forms of psychotherapy, the empowered form serves as the best barometer of defences and resistances.

5. In empowered psychotherapy, the patient is instructed to carry out an adaptive task in each session: to begin with a dream or other narrative and to end with a trigger-decoded insight. Observing how a patient negotiates this responsibility enables the therapist carefully to gauge the extent and nature of the patient's psychological and communicative defences.

6. For this process, the patient must begin the session with an *origination narrative*—a dream or fictional story composed spontaneously in the session. This narrative serves (1) as part of the pool of encoded themes that the patient is obliged to develop and, perhaps more importantly, (2) as the source of *guided associations*—fresh narrative tales that are brought to mind by the elements of the origination narrative and serve to expand the pool of available encoded themes. This pool of derivative themes is constituted as *encoded responses* of the deep unconscious system to the prevailing triggering events within the therapy—primarily the most recent frame-related interventions of the therapist.

7. The ideal self-processing exercise is one in which the patient

carries forward the process to a meaningful deep insight without significantly interfering psychological or communicative defences. To do so, the patient, on his or her own, would carry out the following steps:

a. The presentation of an origination narrative with a notable degree of rich imagery.

b. The development of a pool of encoded narrative themes that embody two essential qualities:

   i. *Frame allusions.* As noted, the deep unconscious system primarily processes frame-related interventions. To be certain that the narrative material reflects deep unconscious processing, then, it should have *bridging themes* that *connect to and represent the currently active frame-related triggers*—the frame-related interventions that the deep unconscious system is processing. Encoded frame themes provide clues to the nature of the trigger and also reflect some of its unconsciously perceived meanings.

   ii. *Power themes.* Power is defined as manifest allusions to *themes of damage*—death, illness, harm, etc.—and of *open sexuality.* The deep unconscious system deals only with triggers and emotional meanings that have been denied and repressed because of their potential to disturb the patient. This means that the system deals only with issues of considerable strength. Strong themes are an indication that the encoded perceptions and processing efforts of the deep unconscious system are represented—no power, no deep unconscious experience.

   In terms of death-related issues, damage themes tend to operate as encoded derivatives of the death-related triggering event, while sexual themes typically represent encoded forms of the denial of death anxiety—a sign that a death-connected triggering event has evoked manic-denial defences.

c. The linking of the encoded themes to their evocative triggers:

   i. This involves the *trigger-decoding process* through which the themes are lifted from their manifest stories and connected to the triggering event—thereby undoing displacement and disguise. The result is an adaptive scenario that utilizes the patient's material exclusively. It begins with the evocative trigger, defines the patient's unconscious experience and processing of the triggering event, and proposes correctives when the trigger is a frame-modifying intervention. In principle, this part of the process can be applied to any form of communicatively oriented therapy.

ii. The trigger-decoded narrative is then used to explain the unconscious meanings of the any existing *patient indicators*—active symptoms, resistances, frame breaks, and the like.

iii. When the trigger is a frame modification, the encoded themes are also used to effect a rectification of the deviant ground rule.

In substance, then, it is possible to characterize the *ideal, trigger-decoding process* as an identified frame-related trigger, a decodable pool of powerful narrative themes, and the linking of the trigger to the themes to reveal the patient's unconscious experience and processing of the triggering event.

Communicative and psychological defences operate (1) by naturally bypassing awareness and nonetheless guiding unconscious processing to the point where unconscious experiences are reflected in encoded derivatives, and (2) by defensively impairing the overall success of the trigger-decoding efforts—usually by interfering with encoded narrative expression or the identification of the most cogent active triggers.

The existence of an ideal decoding process readily facilitates the identification of communicative defences and resistances directed against the overall search for deep understanding. These defences and resistances may be defined as any means by which a patient fails to carry through from an origination narrative to an unconsciously validated trigger-decoded insight.

Using this approach, it is possible to identify a huge lexicon of communicative defences and their psychological counterparts (see chapters 11 and 12). The foundation of these defences is built into the architecture of the emotion-processing mind, and they are therefore universal means of emotional protection. Their use is inevitable, although the specific defences that are unconsciously selected for use by a given patient are individually determined (again, the familiar individuality constrained by universals). In addition, their invocation may extend to inappropriate and excessive usage, thereby creating both resistances within a psychotherapy and emotional dysfunctions in the life of the patient.

* * *

These issues can be illustrated through the clinical example presented above. There are indications there of a likely triggering event in the form of a frame-deviant third-party self-revelation about the therapist and her daughter's illness. If this trigger had in fact been experienced by the patient, *psychologically* it has been either repressed or suppressed for the moment. *Communicatively*, the trigger seems to be reflected in the encoded derivatives contained in the patient's narrative material, but it has been denied manifest expression.

This trigger is sufficient to account for the encoded illness and death themes, not simply as the patient's concern over the health of Dr Tyler's daughter, *but also in terms of the activated experience of a frame-breaking third-party self-revelation*. According to the patient's derivative themes, this frame modification is a destructive, assault-ive, cancerous deviation for which the therapist must bear responsibility, even though she had not herself directly made the break in the frame.

A key point is this: the same encoded narrative embodies communications related to experiences and processes that are under repression in both the superficial unconscious memory subsystem of the conscious system and the memory subsystem of the deep unconscious system. Conscious-system repression is reflected in the thinly disguised encoded representations of the therapist's daughter's illness, while deep unconscious repression is reflected in the more heavily disguised frame-related representations that pertain to the therapist's third-party self-disclosure. Because the encoded meanings of a set of narrative communications are likely to be layered in this fashion, trigger-decoding must consider both levels of unconscious experience. This advice bears repeating, because encoded deep unconscious reactions to the therapist's frame breaks are often overlooked.

Resistances prevail

In the session at hand, Ms Banks' resistances were unusually strong. In the time allotted to her, she was unable to identify an active trigger that could meaningfully account for and be linked to her encoded themes. She also did not present any *indicators* or *self-indicators*, as they are termed in empowered psychotherapy—indications for therapist intervention because of a patient's reported symptoms or frame impingements. Indeed, frame-related activity within the therapy was completely ignored. Without a known and workable trigger, linking is impossible and insight into deep unconscious experience cannot be achieved.

Once the patient's 40-minute effort at self-processing and trigger-decoding was at an end, Dr Tyler intervened with a questioning approach. Her queries were restricted to helping the patient realize that omissions had been made—the patient had not created a list of self-indicators and, more importantly, had not identified an active trigger to account for and link to the encoded themes. These realizations enabled Ms Banks to appreciate that she had been communicatively resistant, and she decided to try to fill in the missing pieces.

Her first thought was that a friend who attends Dr Tyler's church had asked Ms Banks, who is a professional fund-raiser, to join her on the fund-raising committee for the church. In the course of extending the invitation, the friend mentioned the names of other committee members, and this included Dr Tyler.

Ms Banks recognized that this event involved a third-party revelation about the therapist. She also realized that a frame-altering self-indicator of her own was a factor—she had agreed to serve on the committee, thereby creating a situation in which she expected to interact with the therapist outside her office and at a time other than that scheduled for her sessions.

Ms Banks rationalized her decision by arguing that she could be very helpful to the committee and that seeing Dr Tyler at the few meetings of the committee would not be a problem—it might even help the therapist to see how human she is. Beyond that, only one other trigger came to mind—a session that the therapist had cancelled some five weeks earlier.

The patient tried to link these two triggers to the main frame-related themes—primarily, the frame-breaking themes of the affair and its public revelation. She was able to see some connection to the frame-breaking revelation about Dr Tyler being on the fund-raising committee—the outside contact with Dr Tyler might be seen as having an affair with her. It was, however, very difficult to connect this trigger to the *power themes* of assault, cancerous illness, and lasting injury. Assuming that some event must occur to generate such themes, a trigger seemed to be repressed or missing. This likelihood found considerable support in the associated theme of Nan's request that her illness be kept secret. Through this derivative theme, Ms Banks' deep unconscious system evidently was signalling her unconscious need to conceal an emotionally strong triggering event.

The strong signs of *communicative resistance* in this session mainly took the form of obliterating the conscious identification of an active trigger that could account for and be linked to the encoded imagery. Encoded derivatives were available, but not a workable trigger.

Psychologically, this omission might stem from several causes. The patient may have deliberately and consciously decided not to refer to the triggering event. Or unconscious defences may have been used, mainly repression via the forgetting of a known trigger or denial via the failure to recall an event that is so blatant and compelling that its omission has a quality of obliterating an obvious reality. With denial, the links between the encoded imagery and the trigger go unrealized even though they are virtually self-evident. The therapist who is aware of a strong frame-related trigger finds it extremely difficult to understand how the patient could possibly not catch on to the trigger in light of the clarity with which the themes suggest the triggering event. Defences of this kind are not uncommon when the trigger has manifest connections to a death-related event in the life of the therapist.

In developing some ideas about communicative and psychological defences and resistances, we see that the patient's main communicative defence can be precisely specified—it is the failure to achieve a conscious realization of the key trigger. On the other hand, the patient's psychological defences cannot be identified with confidence—they may be operating consciously or unconsciously, or both, and may involve either repression or denial, or both. Even with a direct query of the patient—and this is precluded by principles of technique as it would suggest the nature of the trigger to the patient—some uncertainty would remain.

When it became clear to Ms Banks that her material indicated that there was indeed a missing trigger, she attempted to search for it by invoking direct recall, and by using the available themes as clues to the missing trigger (triggers evoke themes, and therefore themes encode the nature of their triggers).

When Ms Banks searched her memory for an unmentioned trigger, the only thoughts she had were that several months ago she had seen the therapist in church, and a year earlier one of her friends had mentioned that she thought that Dr Tyler had had some kind of surgery during her summer break. These *background triggers* seemed to link to the themes of exposure and illness, so perhaps they had evoked this imagery.

The problem with this conscious self-interpretation is that the deep unconscious system of the emotion-processing mind concentrates its adaptive efforts on the here-and-now situation in terms of currently active frame-related triggering events. Past triggers do not obtain active processing by the deep unconscious system unless they are reactivated by a recently invoked triggering event. This is especially true of current frame-modifying triggers: they consistently call forth past frame deviations for reworking. However, the past trigger cannot be deeply understood without identifying and interpreting (and rectifying to the greatest extent feasible) the contemporary trigger.

The attempt to focus on a past triggering event as a way of avoiding a more immediate trigger is a common communicative defence.

The search for a repressed/denied, communicatively absent but powerful triggering event is among the most difficult tasks in empowered psychotherapy. The unconscious motives for this kind of defence are very strong, and the resistances tend to be sustained for many sessions. When a review of the available themes for clues to the missing trigger does not modify the patient's defensive barriers and prompt the sudden recollection of the missing trigger event, the patient should return to his or her dream or origination story for further guided associations. Doing so provides the deep unconscious system with an opportunity to encode additional clues to the missing triggering event.

This dramatic split in the human mind is characteristic of the functioning of the emotion-processing mind—the deep unconscious system is aware of a trigger, whereas the conscious system is entirely unaware and does not want to know about it at all.

> In the session, Ms Banks drew a blank regarding the missing trigger. She picked up on the themes of church, assault, illness, and cancer, but nothing in the way of an overlooked trigger materialized. Quite spontaneously, however, an odd thought occurred to her. She recalled that she had forgotten that she had promised her friend Nan, the woman who was recovering from uterine cancer, that she would do some shopping for her and spend last Monday night with her. When she failed to show, Nan was forced to go without fresh food and was quite angry with Ms Banks, who was embarrassed and ashamed of her lapse and at a loss to explain it.
>
> Once she finished this story [which is a free rather than a guided association], Ms Banks *brought it into the process;* she tried to decode its meanings by attempting to link the themes to one of the known triggers. All she could do, however, was to see that there was a repetition of the theme of avoidance—avoiding someone with cancer. She had no idea what it meant, but there it was.
>
> Ms Banks next returned to the elements of her dream. She thought of the image of the crutches, which brought to mind a

> short story she had read in her dentist's waiting-room about a physician whose child had become ill. The father felt ashamed of the illness, as if he had failed his son as a medical practitioner in allowing him to become sick. He becomes suicidal in the story, which Ms Banks was unable to finish before she was called in to see the dentist.
>
> Trying to allow these themes to suggest a frame-related trigger was again to no avail. Ms Banks noticed that the theme of illness seemed to be repeating itself, and that there was a reference to doctors, but all she could think of was the old story that the therapist might once have had surgery.
>
> Reviewing these themes for further clues to the missing trigger, Ms Banks failed to recognize consciously the theme of illness in a doctor's child. The session ended with a final story about a news leak that violated a confidential memo sent by a client to his attorney. With her therapist's help, the patient saw that the themes here were of a violated frame and a leaked secret, but still no trigger came to Ms Banks' conscious mind.

It is striking to see how close to a repressed/denied obliterated triggering event a patient can get without the trigger breaking through into awareness. Failing to register key themes consciously when trying to extract critical images and themes from narrative material is another frequently used communicative defence. In this session, even though the derivatives became less and less disguised, the most likely missing trigger—which seems to be the pastor's announcement to the congregation and the patient—still did not occur to the patient consciously. In the "arms race" between defence and deep insight into death-related conflicts, defensiveness seems to prevail again and again.

CONFIRMING THE RESISTANCES

During the week that followed the above session, a friend of Dr Tyler's, who was on the church committee the patient planned to join, referred to the possibility of an outside person joining the committee. Unaware that Ms Banks was Dr Tyler's patient, she referred to her by name and added that she had been at church that Sunday. This confirmed Dr Tyler's impression that Ms Banks was indeed working over the frame-deviant triggering event of the third-party revelation about her daughter.

There are two significant aspects to this active triggering event: (1) the third-party self-revelation, which is a frame deviation that is likely to activate *unconscious* forms of *predatory* forms of death anxiety in the patient, and (2) the nature of the disclosure, which is manifestly death-connected and likely to evoke mainly *conscious and unconscious existential* forms of death anxiety. It is quite common for these two types of stimuli to operate together—a death-related trauma announced through a persecutory frame break.

How, then, did Ms Banks adapt to this information and its meanings? Did she experience this trigger event? And if so, did she experience it consciously and/or unconsciously?

To answer these questions, the observational base and context must be clear. No absolute forms of awareness exist. A patient's awareness depends on the nature of the triggering event and its conscious and unconscious meanings, who is involved in the event, and to whom it is recounted—including both self and others. When an adaptation-evoking trigger involves a patient's therapist, it is processed in ways that are almost always different from how it would be processed if a similar event involves someone else. Furthermore, triggers with a *secured-frame* context will be processed differently from those involving a *modified frame* situation. In attempting to identify the presence of defences and resistances, the status of the frame must be kept in mind.

This instance deals with how a patient adapted to a frame-deviant triggering event that involved her generally frame-securing psychotherapist who had recently modified the frame by cancelling a single session. The nature of the trigger, as well as a therapist's modes of listening and intervening, influence the contents and form of what a patient does and does not communicate in a given session. Narrative material and the conscious identification of active triggers, though emanating from the patient, are products of the patient/therapist system and of the interaction between them. The same principles apply to the therapist, although the outcome of these forces is reflected in ways and forms that are generally different from the patient.

Within this framework, a review of Ms Banks' manifest communications reveals no evidence of immediate conscious awareness of the triggering event. Even though the explorations in the session pointed towards it again and again, there is no direct allusion by Ms Banks to the announcement about her therapist's daughter anywhere in the session.

An analysis from the communicative vantage-point indicates that there are at least four possible explanations for this communicative and psychological void—four possible mechanisms at work. In reviewing them, it will be found that the psychological defences of denial and repression actually have several operative and communicative forms.

1. The first possibility is that the patient was consciously suppressing all references to the trigger, supposedly to spare the therapist emotional pain. This possibility is compatible with this material, but it could be rejected if the patient somehow made it clear that she was not concealing anything.

2. The second possibility is that even though she was present for the sermon, the entire triggering event—that is, the pastor's announcement—failed to register consciously in Ms Banks awareness. This reflects *the psychological defence of denial and the gross communicative defence of non-communication or obliteration*. The defence involves *perceptual denial* because it operated at the perceptual/intake end of the experience. Perceptual denial is a common response to extremely traumatic, death-related, frame-deviant triggers. This defence spares the conscious system an awareness of every aspect of a such an event. However, the defence entails an extreme level of denial and is costly because it precludes any working-over of, and adaptation to, the trauma, whose disruptive effects are sustained unconsciously.

   The use of this defence would be confirmed if the patient was present at the service and nevertheless insisted that she had not heard mention of the therapist's daughter. Even though this denial had been accompanied by disguised encoded images, this defensiveness would be all but impossible to modify through confrontation or interpretation. This form of defence also is compatible with the material to this point in this excerpt.

3. The third possibility is that the appeal by the pastor registered consciously but was then subjected to conscious-system repression. This form of *psychological repression* is the type currently termed *repression* in classical psychoanalytic terms. It involves the non-remembering of an event that has been registered consciously and has then become unavailable to awareness. When recovered, the impression will re-emerge whole cloth, without disguise.

   Communicatively, this type of repression is identified by the absence of direct allusions to the triggering event, by the expression of a number of disguised but decodable, derivative allusions to the trigger, and by a moment when the patient realizes consciously that his or her material is addressing a particular omitted trigger. This form of repression may be moderate, which allows recall after some working through, or severe, which allows recall only after intense and lengthy working through.

   Little or no support is apparent in this material for the operation of moderate repression and temporary non-communication because the patient failed to recover the triggering event despite the working-over of abundant readily decodable derivative images. The interlude to this point does, however, support the possibility of a more severe form of conscious-system repression. The operation of this psychological defence would be confirmed if the patient, after extended effort, eventually recalled the trigger directly and without disguise.

4. The fourth and last possibility is that the triggering event registered consciously but nevertheless ended up in the deep unconscious system and its memory storage subsystem, rather than in the memory storage subsystem of the conscious mind. I term this *post hoc denial* because there is conscious registration and conscious-system processing, but then a shift of the experience out of the conscious system into the deep unconscious system.

> This particular sequence begins with conscious perceptual registration, followed by superficial and then deep-unconscious-system storage and processing, with the result that the trigger can no longer be recovered directly. In this case, there will again be *no direct reference* to the trigger, but there will be a variety of persistent, disguised derivatives (encoded narrative themes). The trigger is *never consciously retrieved by the patient,* but the derivatives the trigger has evoked will continue to be expressed for exceedingly long periods of time—for years in some instances. In this case, the therapeutic work is confined to the encoded material and may meet with some success in alleviating some of the maladaptive consequences of the deeply repressed triggering event. The material of this session is also compatible with this possibility.
>
> The distinction is made between *perceptual denial,* which spares the conscious system all awareness of the trigger, and *post hoc denial,* in which the conscious system experiences a traumatic event but then shuttles the memory of the event into the deep unconscious system. This shift establishes a state of non-awareness of the experience, which can then reach awareness only in encoded form where it must be trigger-decoded. Severe conscious-system repression must also be differentiated from these two sequences. In this last case, a consciously registered triggering event is stored in the superficial unconscious subsystem of the conscious system but then becomes directly available to awareness when the conscious-system repression is modified (see also chapters 11 and 12).

There are many clinical situations in which a therapist is aware of a strong emotionally charged triggering event of which the patient is unaware. The therapist is thereby in a position to observe the vicissitudes of the patient's adaptive efforts—expressive and defensive. Assessment can be made of how the patient handles both the communication of meaningfully representative encoded narratives and the search for the key triggers.

At other times, the therapist is not aware of the central trigger that the patient is working over. This may arise because the therapist has no way of knowing of the trigger—as seen, for example, with a third-party self-revelation of which the therapist is unaware. Or it may occur because the therapist has defensively repressed or obliterated an evocative trigger to which he or she is indeed a party, as seen when a therapist either forgets or fails to recognize the power of a frame-related trigger. When a therapist's defences are active, the encoded themes should be formulated in frame terms to provide clues to the missing trigger to a point where, hopefully, the therapist's defences will be resolved.

* * *

In this clinical situation, defensively Ms Banks' had apparently repressed for the moment both the triggering event (the third-party self-revelation) and its contents. The presence of close (thinly disguised) derivative themes related to both aspects of the triggering event suggest that the patient had experienced the trigger consciously but had repressed both of its aspects. Given the power of the announcement, the likelihood of conscious registration seems great, but at this juncture perceptual denial cannot be eliminated.

The trigger could also have been experienced consciously and then relegated to deep unconscious rather than superficial unconscious processing and storage. The final answer must await the long-term working-over of the trigger until it is seen whether the patient ever consciously recovers the memory of the event on her own (evidence of severe conscious-system repression) or whether it emerges through trigger-decoding by the therapist or not at all (evidence of post hoc, deep unconscious repression). The accuracy of these assessments depends, too, on the therapist's ability to formulate soundly and to trigger-decode the patient's material.

Finally, it can be expected that sustaining her communicative defences and the unconscious perceptions and conflicts aroused by this death-related triggering event would prompt Ms Banks to displace her reactions onto others and possibly to suffer from somatic discharge of this constellation. For example, she might experience severe abdominal symptoms and be convinced that she had cancer—though such would not be the case. Or she would be likely to betray a confidence or become involved in a destructive three-person constellation. These maladaptive actions would be consequences of the deeply denied and repressed unresolved triggering event we have been exploring.

ADAPTING TO A DEATH-RELATED TRIGGER

Clinically, as we have seen, death anxiety manifests itself in patients in two basic forms:

1. *Conscious death anxiety,* which appears as manifest fears of death and dying. This type of death anxiety is, as discussed, either:
   a. well-controlled and transient, or
   b. persistent and morbid, *mortophobia.*
2. *Unconscious death anxiety,* which manifests itself through symptoms and behaviours that can be linked through trigger-decoding to death-related issues. The key to identifying this form of death anxiety lies with discovering its adaptation-evoking triggers and decoding the available encoded themes in light of that event.

In general, these unconscious responses are maladaptive because they are driven by unconscious anxieties and result in dysfunctional symptoms and behaviours. However, we should be clear that the invocation of mental defences against the disruptive effects of death anxiety, no matter how obliterating, are not necessarily maladaptive. The adaptive effectiveness of a given patient's defences can be assessed only in light of his or her actual behaviours and the presence or absence of symptomatic, maladaptive phenomena—intrapsychic and interpersonal.

The triggering events for the emergence of these anxieties in patients may take place within or outside therapy. Nevertheless, unconscious forms of death anxiety tend to be triggered by frame-related interventions by therapists, and outside triggers tend to evoke conscious forms of death anxiety. However, these external events tend to link up in crucial ways with triggers from within the treatment situation. Thus, even when the external evocative event is self-evident, as in the case of the death of someone important to a patient, there typically are unconscious sources of the resultant death anxieties, especially when they persist.

The unconscious experiences and meanings that tend to evoke conscious death anxiety include actual life-endangering threats and the full range of possible death-connected events. In contrast, unconscious forms of death anxiety stem from such experiences as unconscious perceptions of murderous wishes in someone else directed towards the patient (and this can include the therapist), frame-management activities (securing or modifying), and all manner of non-death moments that remind a patient of his or her personal mortality.

Whatever the trigger and its meanings, the responsive death anxiety may be felt directly or be relegated to unconscious experience. In empowered psychotherapy, where these issues can be explored in some detail, it has been found that the conscious obliteration of death-evoking triggers and activated death anxieties is extremely common—unconscious forms of death anxiety are far more prevalent than are conscious forms.

The search for death-activating triggers and death-related encoded narratives is therefore an ever-present task in all types of psychotherapy, even though these are very difficult to detect without the use of the communicative approach and trigger-decoding. Empowered psychotherapy facilitates this pursuit, and it can be used by any therapist who is prepared to master the adaptive listening process of the communicative approach and its culmination in trigger-decoding. Then, and only then, does the full and remarkably diverse range of manifestations of patients' death anxieties become visible.

CHAPTER TEN

Selection principles and mental defences

The communicative approach; with its adaptive orientation and use of trigger-decoding, calls for revisions and extensions of current understanding and formulation of mental and behavioural defences. As defined in chapter 1, *mental defences* are all non-action, non-somatic protective measures adopted by the human mind as adaptive or maladaptive responses to disturbing adaptation-evoking triggering events. While these defences do have complex behavioural consequences, they operate primarily in the psychological sphere.

The two basic forms of human *mental defences* are:

1. *Active (non-avoidance) coping efforts.* This includes all measures taken by humans to deal actively with an emotionally charged triggering event—something akin to the fight aspect of adaptation as defined by Cannon (1929). For example, were a therapist to say something nasty to a patient, an active mental coping response might involve the patient's consciously working over the experience in his or her mind. Quite often, this mental

coping effort would lead to an active communicative (and behavioural) reaction as well. For example, the patient might confront the therapist with his or her nastiness, leave therapy, or take other measures to redress the situation.

Humans have a wide range of active mental coping resources, individually crafted from the universal attributes of the emotion-processing mind. Most active responses to triggers are orchestrated by the conscious system and involve conscious perception, thought, and communication, which tend to be heightened when used actively—rather than diminished as they are with avoidance defences (see below).

2. *Avoidance coping efforts.* These mental efforts are modelled on the flight form of adaptation described by Cannon (1929). It is the psychological aspects of this group of defences first defined by Freud (1915d, 1923b, 1926d [1925]), which have subsequently been elaborated by later-day analysts (e.g. Arlow & Brenner, 1964; Dorpat, 1985; A. Freud, 1936). Defences such as denial and repression are obliterating or avoidance mechanisms, although some forms of these mechanisms, repression more than denial, allow for disguised or encoded representations of the obliterated triggering event and its meanings—the classical concept of compromise and the return of the repressed in defensive formations.

In addition to the many psychological defences identified by various psychoanalysts, there is a vast array of communicative mental avoidance defences as well. As we saw in chapter 9, they involve a great variety of ways that patients find to avoid completing a self-processing exercise, which begins with an origination narrative and ends with a trigger-decoded deep insight and, when necessary, a sound frame-management response.

Avoidance defences protect the individual, but they also entail loss of information and meaning useful and often vital for successful adaptation. They are a basis for maladaptation, interpersonal disturbance, and psychopathology because these defences do not allow for the proper conscious processing of and adaptation to triggering events. They remove from awareness many of the disturbing meanings and effects of triggers, but thereby they promote dysfunctional displacements from the source of the adaptive issue to elsewhere. In addition, the unconsciously experienced meanings of the triggering event persist in the two unconscious systems of the emotion-processing mind—the superficial unconscious subsystem of the conscious system and the wisdom and fear–guilt subsystems of the deep unconscious system. So placed, these constellations unconsciously wreak havoc with a person's emotional life and behaviours. They are inaccessible to change unless trigger-decoding is brought to bear on the encoded narratives generated by these unconscious constellations.

For ease of discussion, I will hereafter use the term "defence" to refer to avoidance mental defences and behavioural reactions, unless otherwise specified. It is the avoidance aspect of defence that is, after all, most responsible for emotional maladaptations.

SOME FRESH LEADS

It is of some relevance to our full appreciation of the nature of mental defences to understand the source of the inspiration for the fresh views on this subject. These ideas began to emerge as the communicative approach itself evolved, but they materialized in more definitive form when the architecture and operations of the emotion-processing mind, and their evolutionary history, were subjected to investigation and clarification (Langs, 1995, 1996).

In this context, the main impetus for these insights arose from the study of how the emotion-processing mind operates as a cognitive mental module with regard to immediate efforts at adaptation. Adaptation implies coping, and it has two components:

1. primarily creative adaptive responses;
2. primarily protective adaptive responses.

In time, it became clear that the emotion-processing mind has been shaped in large measure as a protective cognitive module for which creativity is a secondary accomplishment. It is shaped more by trauma than support, and it is activated more by disturbance than by care.

These ideas drew their leads from studies of our primary adaptive and protective *physical resources*—the *human brain* and *immune system*. These organ systems are activated by disturbing animate and inanimate environmental impingements and disruptive internal physical stimuli, much as the emotion-processing mind is activated by emotionally charged events. While the human *brain* appears inherently to have both creative and defensive potential, a great deal of which is expressed through the cognitive *mind, the immune system essentially is an evolved defensive system.*

These physical entities operate as so-called *Darwin machines* (Plotkin, 1994), which function according to the principles of *universal Darwinism* (Dawkins, 1983). In essence, this means that they operate according to rules of *selection* rather than those of *instruction;* environmental impingements select responses from available resources rather than instructing the organism how to respond.

For example, Edelman (1987, 1992) has argued that environmental events *select,* from available assets, those existing tracts, interconnections, and modules of the pre-wired inherited *brain* that are most responsive and adaptive to the prevailing activating events. A given incident does not instruct or direct the brain to react in a particular way—a response that would be rigidly reinforced through principles of learning. Instead, the brain *as inherited,* contains a huge number of pre-formed and flexible resources. Specific experiences then operate on the brain to select those brain resources and configurations that are most effectively responsive to the environmental event. The brain's pre-wired perceptual capacities play a role in this selectivity, as does its existing architecture. Operating according to these principles, the brain is not enslaved to the environment; its capabilities are selected for response, and once a response has been effected, it has the potential to self-organize in creative ways that enhance one's adaptive capabilities.

Using these ideas to direct the search, evidence was soon accumulated that the human emotion-processing mind operates according to selection principles that are similar to its substrate, the human brain. This idea was further reinforced by investigations of the adaptive strategies of the immune system.

In the 1950s, Burnet (1959) and then Jerne (1967; see also Gazzaniga, 1992; Langs, 1996) were able to show that the human immune system also does not operate, as was supposed, in instructionistic fashion. That is, the old theory proposed that an environmental event, like the entry into the bloodstream of a micro-organism, a so-called *antigen*, evoked a reading by the blood system which then, as per instructions from the micro-organism, designed and manufactured a responsive *antibody* created to destroy the antigen.

In contrast, the revised and currently accepted theory is that the human body has, by inherited design, some 40 to 60 billion different antibodies circulating as lymphocytes in the bloodstream. When an antigen enters the bloodstream, it causes the favoured reproduction of the antibody or antibodies that will best operate to destroy it. These antibodies then reproduce or proliferate favourably and eradicate the invading organism, combining in creative ways to be optimally effective. In addition, lymphocytes retain a *memory marker* after the invading antigen has been eliminated. If the antigen or a close copy returns as an invader, the response is more rapid and extensive than before—effective adaptation and defence has been programmed and becomes more efficient.

Two major developments in the theoretical edifice of the communicative approach were derived from these explorations. The first is the concept that the emotion-processing mind, as a basic emotionally adaptive human resource, must operate according to selectionistic principles. And the second is that mental defences must be based on a huge resource and that these defences must, like the huge variety of brain and immune-system defensive resources, exist in very large numbers.

SELECTIONISM AND THE EMOTION-PROCESSING MIND

The thesis that the emotion-processing mind must operate according to selectionistic principles is grounded on the repeated observation that nature and natural selection conserve their designs and resources. Once engineered and evolved, models tend to be reused with necessary modifications wherever they can prove to be serviceable in fresh contexts. This rule is illustrated in the finding that our two basic systems for coping with environmental threat—the brain and the immune system—both operate according to selectionist principles. Compared to instructionistic adaptations, selectionistic forms of coping are energically costly because they require the development of vast inner resources. But the trade-off is that selectionism allows for much more effective and flexible means of coping and surviving than does instructionism.

The *human mind*, and its emotion-processing component, is another fundamental organ of adaptation to and protection from disturbing environmental impingements. Indeed, it is the mind supported by the brain that carries out most emotional adaptations. It was therefore expected that the emotion-processing mind also operates according to selectionist principles as a Darwin machine (Langs, 1996). A fresh look at the therapeutic interaction and at the adaptations of patients and therapists in this light, including a re-evaluation of the operations of mental defences, strongly supported this proposition.

It appears, then, that emotionally charged environmental impingements select from a given individual's inherited and developmentally enhanced mental resources those responses that are best designed to cope with the nature and meanings of the event. Once chosen, this response is favourably reproduced and recorded in a memory storage system. Later, whenever a similar event occurs, the response, now enhanced, will be called forth.

* * *

In elaborating on this proposition, three problems emerged.

The first pertains to the available adaptive capacities of the emotion-processing mind. As is true of all coping systems, there is a limitation to the amount and intensity of environmental input that the system can, through selectionism, process successfully. Impingements may be so repetitive or severely traumatic that they overwhelm the resourcefulness of the system. The result will be system overload and maladaptive responses.

In addition to this, according to the rules of selectionism, once selected, the automatic tendency is to repeat the maladaptive reaction under similar circumstances. A long evolutionary heritage favours the search for similarities among traumatic triggering events—for example, to take flight from larger predators. This means that selected responses, even when maladaptive, will tend to be called forth to respond to broader and broader categories of events, and eventually include events in which the differences from the original traumas are significant, but subjugated to the fewer similarities. In essence, the emotion-processing mind *overgeneralizes* in its applications of selected defensive adaptations to the point at times of fundamental error and maladaptation.

The second problem arises because the emotion-processing mind has evolved to favour avoidance defences over active coping defences in response to emotionally charged triggers. The emergence of language capabilities and the clear definition of death-related triggering events created selection pressures that played a major role in this preference, which reflects one of several major design flaws in the architecture of the emotion-processing mind. The result is a natural preference for maladaptive defensively avoidant selections, which are then repeated when comparable stimuli occur. This makes the selection process quite troublesome for emotional life and creates a significant challenge for the psychotherapies that are offered to set matters right.

The third difficulty arises from the problems inherent to modifying selected coping responses when they essentially are costly and maladaptive. Selection principles tend to lead to fixed choices, and these responses are seldom modified in existing organisms. Evolutionary change requires a new generation with fresh variants on which the selection process can operate over long periods of time. It is therefore difficult for an individual who has made unconscious selections to change these choices, even when they cause suffering and even with favourable changes in environmental conditions.

* * *

Instructionism can have some power to change conscious-system selections, as witnessed by conditioning and deconditioning and similar forms of therapy. It cannot, however, affect unconscious processes that are inaccessible to consciously stated external directives. Modifying unconscious defences involves the rather difficult problem of how to alter maladaptive selections or replace them with more adaptive ones. The solution to this critical question has proven to be elusive.

Mental defences have both phylogenetic and ontogenetic sources. Phylogenetically, the available armamentarium for defending against the hurtful consequences of emotional trauma and death-related events has, as noted, tended to favour avoidance defences and denial in particular. Ontogenetically, the actual mobilization and success or failure of individually selected defences depends on the frequency and intensity of a person's experience with death-connected events and the nature of his or her inherited resources. Once selected, however, the defences the individual develops early in life tend to persist in relatively unmodified form. It is these defences and their effects that emerge in the course of a psychotherapy.

For example, if the primary defensive reactions to early death-related traumas are those of active coping, future reactions are likely to be similar. On the other hand, if the response is to be overwhelmed and overly defensive, this pattern will be repeated again and again in the life of the individual. Given that most of these selection events occur in infancy and early childhood, the conditions favour avoidance defence over creative active coping. In addition to the general helplessness experienced in dealing with death, the young child is in a weak and vulnerable position vis-à-vis the environment. Despite later changes in coping capacities, these maladaptive preferences tend to persist.

The issue for the psychotherapist is, then, how to modify effectively a patient's maladaptive defensive selections. In light of the prevalence of selectionism in this area, this problem calls for something more than effective trigger-decoded interpretations and frame-securing interventions. While these techniques have favourable effects, they do not seem to be capable of modifying the basic design of the emotion-processing mind. And it is this design in particular that needs favourable changing if we are to adapt more effectively to our existential death anxieties and to the specific death-related events that arise in the course of everyone's life.

THE MULTIPLICITY OF DEFENCES

The second theoretical development to arise from studies of the immune system and brain came from the realization that the human brain and immune system have a huge number, evidently in the millions, of actual and potential adaptive and defensive resources. The hypothesis, then, is that much the same should apply to the emotion-processing mind. This cognitive/adaptive module is likely to possess a huge repertoire of mental defences—far greater in number than the handful that have been identified until now.

The brain and immune systems have had millions of years in which to evolve in other species as well as in our own. In contrast, the language-based, emotion-processing mind has had a mere 100,000–150,000 years to develop. Nevertheless, nature's rule of conserving patterns of resource suggested the search for a more complete armamentarium of defences against environmental traumas than currently known.

The first impression that encouraged this search was that the emotion-processing mind as presently configured appears to be primarily a defensively oriented system. An analogy between the human mind and human blood suggested itself. In addition to lymphocytes and other components of the immune system, the blood contains elements like haemoglobin for carrying oxygen and platelets for clotting. Similarly, in addition to its defences, the emotion-processing mind has elements that assist creativity, taking care of our personal and survival needs and the like. Clinical observations show, nevertheless, that the defensive operations of the emotion-processing mind appear to be its main function.

This suggests another way—in addition to the separation of the conscious and deep unconscious systems—of organizing the adaptive functions of the emotion-processing mind. For this kind of exploration, this cognitive module would be separated into two basic subsystems—one for the creative satisfactions of human needs and the other for defending against disruptive environmental and internal impingements. These two aspects of the operations of the emotion-processing mind would each rely on contributions from the conscious and deep unconscious systems. In this way, the huge amount of structure and energy that is devoted to defensive operations within and by the emotion-processing mind might find further illumination.

The avoidance defensive posture of the emotion-processing mind appears to be an evolved, universal attribute and the predominant modus operandi of its several systems. Much like the immune system, the module is designed to defend against predators—physical, psychological, and emotional. And, again like the immune system, the primary threat for the system is death-related—microbes in one case, emotional events (often with physical underpinnings) with meanings linked to death in the other.

Death anxiety appears to have played a major role in the evolution and current architecture of the emotion-processing mind and is accountable for its largely defensive posture. On the most fundamental level, the defences of the emotion-processing mind, psychological and communicative, are configured to protect the individual against overly disruptive forms of this type of anxiety.

Given the limited number of *psychological defences* that have been identified in the first hundred years of thinking, the search for the multiple and diverse defensive resources of the emotion-processing mind focused on *communicative defensiveness*. While psychological defences operate intrapsychically and interpersonally with respect to repressed and disowned mental contents, communicative defences operate entirely through language and entail efforts to disguise or obliterate unconscious experience as reflected in communicated messages.

Clinical work—especially within empowered psychotherapy, where communicative defences are most readily identified—has revealed a large and varied repertoire of these defences. Evidence also has accumulated that death anxiety is a major motivator for their invocation, especially when the defensiveness appears to be virtually intractable. Once the concept of *communicative defence* had been formalized, the following points became clear:

1. There are indeed many communicative defences.
2. They are primarily of the avoidance type; they disguise and obliterate the unconsciously registered meanings of emotionally charged experiences and prevent the emergence of trigger-decoded insights.

3. They appear to be more fundamental than psychological defences in that a single psychological defence tends to resolve into a variety of communicative defences.

4. Communicative and psychological mental defences are different levels and means of defending against anxiety-provoking impingements, especially those that evoke the various types of death anxiety. The recognition of each type of defence depends on a therapist's methods of listening, formulating, and intervening. An appreciation of the nature of unconscious communication is essential for the identification of the communicative type of defence.

5. Both classes of defence are based on design features and unconscious psychodynamic forces, including conflicts involving death anxiety. However, the clinical approach to resolving these two forms of defence are quite different. Psychological defences are identified by inference on the basis of their indirect effects, and they may be modified through confrontation or some forms of interpretation.

   On the other hand, the obliterating types of communicative defence can be identified directly and conscious efforts made to modify them—for example, by supplying a missing triggering event so that linking with themes can be accomplished. Still, with both types of defence, modifying their continued use proves difficult, especially when death-related issues are involved.

* * *

Let us now take a closer look at these mental defences and their supportive partner—behavioural forms of defence.

CHAPTER ELEVEN

Psychological defences

In this and the next chapter, I offer a reconsideration of mental defences. I begin by identifying the major motives for defence formation, then present a recasting of the nature of psychological defences, catalogue currently known communicative defences, and show the relationship of communicative defences to psychological defences on the one hand, and behavioural defences on the other. The role of death anxiety in these processes and relationships is an ever-present consideration.

THE MOTIVES FOR DEFENCE

The design of the emotion-processing mind, individually configured within well-defined constraints, is universal. Similarly, both the general adaptive resources and the protective avoidance defences used in the emotional realm are activated by basic universal motives. Historically, these needs and motives were subject to natural selection, and they then shaped the structure and operations of the emotion-processing mind. They continue to do so each day throughout the life of a given individual.

Several principal conscious and unconscious motivationally selective forces play a role in the development of the individually honed defences of the emotion-processing mind.

1. *Specific emotionally traumatic environments and events, and their immediate and cumulative effects*

The emotion-processing mind has selectively evolved to deal with environmental impingements, which, in turn, affect its architecture, motivations, and coping preferences. These events and interpersonal transactions are impact-laden triggers, as are the particular physical and psychological boundaries, rules, and settings within which they occur. They may be of a positive and gratifying nature, or negative, traumatic, and death-related.

In a manner not unlike the immune system, the emotion-processing mind is more deeply affected by traumatic experiences than it is by supportive, nurturing, gratifying events. Emotionally disturbing events/traumas create intrapsychic motives within the individual and configure the defensive design of the emotion-processing mind. While harmful agents and events give form and intensity to the defences used by a given person, positive experiences largely create the backdrop or context within which defences can be utilized in a more successful manner. The stronger the supportive environment, the more adaptive the mental defences used by a given individual. Poor environmental conditions promote fragile, over-intense, and maladaptive defences.

Emotionally charged traumatic events and messages embody and impart both conscious and unconscious meanings. These meanings are received as such, but they are also subjected to internal selection and shaping processes with respect to both conscious and unconscious experience. The net result is largely faithful to the realities of the event, but particular meanings are emphasized, in keeping with the inner dynamic state of the emotion-processing mind. Distortion and misperception do occur, but they tend to involve the conscious rather than the deep unconscious system.

Both the openness and the defensiveness of the emotion-processing mind play a role in emotional experience. There are key points at which inner influence is notable. This includes the perceptual level, where perceptual defences may lead to a partial or entirely obliterated experience of the event. Defences also may operate in both the conscious and deep unconscious systems, thereby influencing both conscious and unconscious experience. The assessment of the traumatic power of a given incident must take into account all of these aspects of an event. This entails an appreciation of the severity of the actual happening was well as the individual's sensitivities, based largely on his or her trauma and death-related histories and coping resources.

Death-related traumas evoke forms of predatory or traumatic death anxiety and are most critical in selectively shaping the defensive structure of the emotion-processing mind. Given the relative inability actively to affect the course of these traumas and the relatively few available adaptive solutions to the anxieties evoked by death-related events, these experiences evoke considerable helplessness. Active coping is either impossible or likely to fail. *These realities favour the selection and repetition of obliterating defences rather than active coping efforts.*

2. *Awareness of the inevitability of death for oneself and others*

Existential death anxiety also plays a role in the motivations for mental defence. This language-based awareness develops in early childhood and is with us until life's end—it is the backdrop of death anxiety upon which predatory death-related events have their effects. Because no adaptive effort can fully resolve this issue, this awareness motivates and favours the use of obliterating defences rather than active coping.

3. *Interpersonal conflict*

This factor is a critical variant of external trauma that affects the selected development of inner motivations for defence and the shaping of the emotion-processing mind. For example, parents will communicate a wide range of conscious and especially unconscious cues to children as to the kinds of behaviours and communications that are acceptable and unacceptable. When an unacceptable impulse arises and it is associated with punishment, an interpersonal conflict will develop, which selects for interceding defences. The child then generalizes these unconsciously applied strictures and applies them to a variety of analogous situations and people in inappropriate and maladaptive fashion. Because of the child's relatively weak position, obliterating defences are favoured rather than active, adaptive confrontations and other active coping efforts. At every turn, obliterating, barrier, and exclusionary defences are preferred to those that would allow for conscious awareness and active negotiation.

4. *Intrapsychic conflicts that motivate defence formations*

These are the inner mental conflicts that pit, for example, a child's instinctual drive wishes towards individuals like his or her parents against the superego strictures that forbid them. In these situations, interpersonal conflicts have been internalized and expanded into internal warfare. Given that the wishes, needs, impulses, and fantasies that are causing these conflicts are dangerous and forbidden, once again obliterating defences tend to be greatly preferred in selecting for responses to specific situations. Inner conflicts aroused by activated death anxieties are of significance in the motivating forces created in this manner.

* * *

A review of the motivating forces that select and shape the emotion-processing mind's structure and adaptive processing efforts leads to the inevitable conclusion that the environmental events that are the determinants of these mental developments strongly press all humans towards an armamentarium of obliterating defences as a necessity in coping with emotional life. There is a hint here, too, that finding ways to affect the design of the emotion-processing mind that favour active coping would be extremely helpful not only in psychotherapy, but in everyday life as well. The problem lies with discovering effective techniques with which to achieve this goal—it requires a monumental change in the design of the operations of the emotion-processing mind.

PSYCHOLOGICAL DEFENCES

Clinical studies using the communicative approach indicate that *denial and repression* are the basic form and foundation for all psychological defences. Both are obliterating in their effects. Although these defences operate in the mind of a given individual, they are under the constant influence of interactional, interpersonal, setting, and ground-rule/contextual factors. They are not static or isolated intrapsychic operations, but are ongoing aspects of continuing adaptations. The force and nature of events and relationships may change their status at any given moment. In a sense, then, all psychological defences are interactional and interpersonal, regardless whether they are defined in internal terms, like repression and denial, or in interpersonal terms, like projective identification.

Manifestations of defences are both similar and different in form for patients and for therapists, in keeping with their role requirements, behavioural and communicative opportunities, and general constraints within the therapeutic interaction. The main psychological defences of the emotion-processing mind appear to be:

1. *Denial.* This defence operates intrapsychically, with dramatic effects on one's experience of the environment (Dorpat, 1985). It is the fundamental obliterating defence; it eradicates and falsifies reality and involves gross misperceptions and erroneous beliefs. While initially considered to be a psychotic defence in that it generally entails a break with reality, we now know that there are non-psychotic forms of this defence that may be neurotic or even healthy, as seen with an ongoing denial of death that does not put an individual at risk or render him or her emotionally maladaptive.

Denial is the primary defence against death anxiety. Existential death anxiety in particular has served as a major selection factor for the uniquely human development of this defence. Denial is, however, also brought into play in the presence of predatory death-related events, often to great disadvantage.

Adaptation is in general served by heightened sensitivity to environmental and internal threat. Denial reduces this sensitivity and entails significant levels of knowledge reduction, and therefore appears to be an unusual type of obliterating defence, exquisitely selected to deal with the singular human awareness of ultimate demise. While denial is always costly, it is especially maladaptive when it is overused and/or applied to situations where its invocation unduly interferes with sound responsiveness. The potential for this type of difficulty is seen in the many ways that the reality of death as the end of life is denied—for example, belief in an afterlife and in communication with those who have died.

Communicatively, denial is thought to obliterate all representations of the denied event. However, as we shall see, a more refined approach to this defence shows this not to be the case—denied triggers and their meanings are often encoded in patients' communications. Thus, denied experiences are afforded encoded representation, but they do not yield readily to trigger-decoding and conscious realization.

2. *Repression.* While denial tends to be seen as the primary defence against traumatic environmental impingements, repression has mainly been thought of as the primary defence against anxiety-provoking, conflictual inner fantasies, wishes, and memories—including meanings of death-related events. So defined, repression entails the failure to consciously recall or remember these inner contents lest they evoke anxiety and superego punishment. More recently, repression has been thought of as an interactional and relational mechanism through which aspects of the self and various kinds of impulses towards others that are unconsciously forbidden or objected to by important others are barred from awareness (Slavin & Kriegman, 1992).

In essence, then, repression is defined as the obliteration of inner fantasies and self-aspects and it is seen as operating under interactional conditions. In addition, repression is effected by defensive barriers that are subject to modification by various means, so that repressed contents are allowed entry into awareness—for example, the resolution of the underlying conflicts, a jarring loose by later comparable experiences, confrontation, interpretation, and the like.

Just as the interventions that modify repressive defences are difficult to define, the identification of the actuality of a repressive barrier is also difficult to establish with any degree of precision. In the usual psychodynamic approach, the evidence for repressed contents within a patient relies heavily on many arbitrary clinical judgements that would be all but impossible to validate.

Repression operates to interfere with the recall of death-related experiences and their most devastating meanings, and of the recognition of one's own violent and murderous impulses. Evolved largely to deal with death anxiety, repression of death-related conflicts is a central function of this mental mechanism.

Communicatively, repressed contents are understood to return to awareness in compromised form. This is the basis for Freud's concept of derivatives, which he defined as disguised expressions of unconscious fantasies and memories. However, the specific nature and the vicissitudes of derivative communication have not been explored to any notable extent.

3. *Projection.* This psychological defence has its foundation in both denial and repression. It is defined as an unconscious mechanism through which self-attributes like fantasies, wishes, needs, impulses, and the like are denied or repressed and then attributed to another person. Predatory death-related impulses are often projected onto others.

4. *Reaction formation.* This defence is based on repression and denial, and it operates by turning a particular wish or impulse into its opposite.

5. *Undoing.* This defence may operate either psychologically or

behaviourally. It, too, is based on repression and denial, and it entails the expression of a given impulse, usually aggressive but sometimes sexual, and then obliterating or reversing its meanings, existence, or effects.

6. *Isolation.* This defence supports repression by separating a fantasy from its affect, or a wish from its object.
7. *Identification.* This mechanism is often seen as growth-promoting and therefore actively adaptive on a psychological level. But it also can be invoked defensively as a means of becoming like someone else in order to undo an experience of loss or as a means of gaining strength and denying helplessness, as seen in identification with the aggressor.
8. *Splitting.* This is a mental mechanism that supports repression and at times denial by dividing up into separate segments one's images and experiences of self or others, or of a traumatic event and its meanings.
9. *Introjective identification.* This defence is one of a group of defences that introduce active interactional transactions into defensive operations. Thus, these psychological mechanisms do not simply operate within the individual's mind under interactional influence. Instead, they entail defence formations that appear to be psychologically based actions. Introjective identification is therefore an interactional means of actively taking on the attributes of another person—the effects are both behavioural and psychological.
10. *Projective identification.* This interactional defence involves unconscious efforts to place one's own mental contents and states into another person.

In general, psychological defences are a mixed group of protective mechanisms that operate on, influence, and describe mental states, inner mental operations, and interpersonal transactions. These defences tend to make contents unavailable to the conscious mind. They operate automatically and are unconsciously motivated, but they are exceedingly difficult to identify precisely in the clinical situation. They tend, however, to be generally obliterating in nature and to have a wide range of mental and behavioural effects.

They are supplemented with consciously invoked mental defences like manifest avoidance, suppression, and the like, which have less power and influence than do those that operate unconsciously.

Communicatively, psychological defences tend to affect the contents of a patient's material and to cause gross distortions, omissions, and disguised expressions. However, therapeutic work tends to be concentrated on accessing the repressed or denied contents rather than on an exploration and modification of the communicative obstacles per se.

DEFINING DEFENCES

Psychological defences operate on mental contents, impulses, states, interactional pressures and transactions, and selfhood. They are mental mechanisms that tend to modify these psychological factors internally and interpersonally in ways that render certain anxiety-provoking contents and pressures absent from conscious awareness. In contrast, *communicative defences* operate on the expression of these inner states and interactional pressures in terms of language representations and their vicissitudes. The key difference lies with the *mental operations* of the first group of defences and the *communicative operations* of the second group.

The underlying contents, meanings, and forces that are at issue and call for realizations regarding the environment and emotional life—conflicts, urges, and such—are the same for both types of mental defence. The two domains reflect different perspectives on the same phenomena, which, with respect to mental defence, involve unconscious efforts to disown and obliterate disturbing experiences of the environment and self in the course of moment-to-moment transactions and efforts at adaptation.

In general, the definition of psychological defences is difficult and uncertain, although the stimuli, perceptions, and conflicts that are the basis for these defences may with some effort prove to be identifiable. The subjective judgement of therapists plays a significant role in these assessments, because their evaluations rely on their view of reality (as in the case of denial), memory (as in the case of repression), their own behaviour and interventions (as in the case of projection and projective identification), and the like.

To be accurate, the identification of a psychological defence should begin with the adaptation-evoking triggering event for the invocation of the defence and not rely on isolated speculations regarding intrapsychic happenings. Much the same applies to communicative defences: their definition must begin with a recognition of the trigger and a tracing of the individual's communicative responses from there. However, even though subjective judgement comes into play here too, the identification of the presence of a communicative defence is based on clearer criteria than those that apply to psychological defences.

The communicative approach has with some degree of precision identified the communicative path from a triggering event and its unconscious consequences to the conscious realization of the anxiety-provoking meanings of that event. Therapists can ascertain relatively easily whether a frame-related triggering event has or has not been alluded to by the patient. Similarly, there are clear criteria for encoded expression and for the presence of definitive unconscious meaning in a patient's material—both power and frame themes must be present. As a result, the existence and nature of defensive operations are easier to identify with communicative defences than is the case with the psychological group. With this in mind, we turn now to a more thorough look at communicative defences.

CHAPTER TWELVE

Communicative defences

The standard against which communicative defences can be identified involves two possible *open, non-defensive communicative sequences*. They are:

1. *Conscious registration*, followed by direct or language-based awareness and responsiveness.
2. *Unconscious registration*, followed by encoded language-based representation, the identification of the evocative triggering event, and then trigger-decoding so that the unconscious experience is brought into conscious awareness.

In principle, then, *communicative defensiveness* following conscious registration is defined as a failure to sustain awareness of a previously registered, consciously experienced event and its meanings. Psychologically, this would be termed *conscious-system repression* because the defence operates in the realm of conscious experience; communicatively, it would be identified as *conscious-system non-communication*.

With respect to unconscious registration, communicative defensiveness has two major forms. The first involves the natural use of encoding or disguise, with the resultant creation of derivative representations. Depending on its consequences, this process may be adaptive or maladaptive. The second form is, however, always maladaptive to some degree; it entails the obstruction of the trigger-decoding process.

FACTORS IN COMMUNICATIVE DEFENSIVENESS

The architecture and adaptive resources of the emotion-processing mind are such that there is an in-built communicative defensive alignment that supports the maintenance of undecoded derivatives and opposes their proper decoding. These defences materialize whenever a patient attempts to pursue the trigger-decoding of his or her responses to currently active and compelling emotionally charged trigger events. Communicative defence rather than open communication is the norm for deep unconscious experience.

Communicative defences are universal by design, but under the added influence of psychodynamic factors. They are inevitably activated when the emotion-processing mind strives to adapt to and defend itself against disturbing emotional impingements by relegating critical meanings of the event to unconscious perception and deep unconscious processing.

These defences, even when they are avoidant and obliterating, are not inherently pathological or maladaptive. There is an ever-present trade-off between the effects of the awareness of the disturbing meanings of an emotionally charged triggering event and the absence of such awareness. In the emotional domain, awareness can at times be more disruptive than non-awareness. This attribute of emotional knowing seems to have been a major selection pressure for natural selection, which has, to date, consistently favoured loss of knowledge over its gain in the emotional realm. Even though eradication of emotional experience means that active coping efforts, true resolution of conflict and disturbance, and the expansion of adaptive resources are precluded, its use may still be the best option under given circumstances. This is especially true of death-related triggering events whose emotional implications may be devastating.

The selection of particular communicative defences is, however, an individual characteristic. Individual choice constrained by the universal design of the emotion-processing mind is the essence of the situation. Each person's preferred defensive armamentarium is a result of both ontogeny and phylogeny—genetically inherited and personal developmental factors. Death-related adaptive issues play a role on both levels.

Clinical experience has shown that the selected alignment of communicative defences adopted by a given patient is an attribute that is rather fixed and characteristic of the individual. Changing a patient's communicative style and alignment of communicative defences is extremely difficult. These attributes are based on inherited structures and traumatic events that leave lasting residuals. The power of the protection offered by communicative defences is such that they are seldom surrendered.

Most psychotherapy patients reveal maladaptive or dysfunctional communicative tendencies. They tend excessively to obliterate triggers that are critical to their emotional lives or to be sparse in expressing derivative themes through their narratives. They also strongly resist linking triggers to themes in order to render deep unconscious meanings conscious. It therefore follows that helping patients to communicate more meaningfully and to be capable of their own trigger-decoding would be highly ameliorative.

As yet we lack the definitive techniques through which this can be accomplished. Positive experiences, frame-securing efforts, and trigger-decoded interpretations yield meaningful deep insights, but they generally do not alter a patient's basic, defensive communicative style. In contrast, trauma does strongly affect the defensive alignment of the emotion-processing mind and an individual's use of maladaptive communicative defences. In particular, death-related traumas almost always intensify and harden the use of communicative defences in ways that are difficult to reverse. The vicissitudes of communicative defences and efforts to render them more flexible and less obliterating so patients can accomplish trigger-decoding when needed are prime concerns of the psychotherapist.

SOME CLINICALLY IDENTIFIED COMMUNICATIVE DEFENCES

To focus on communicative defences related to deep unconscious experience, we may establish the specific form of relatively defence-free communication. This sequence is seen most clearly in empowered psychotherapy and entails the following steps:

1. The initiation of communication with the report of an *origination narrative*—a dream or fictional story made up at the start of the session.
2. The creation of a *pool of encoded themes* via narrative guided associations to the origination narrative. This network must have both frame allusions (clues and bridges to the triggering events) and *power* (themes of damage or overt sexuality); it must also have the potential to be meaningfully linked to the currently activating triggers.
3. The identification of *self-indicators*, mainly the patient's impingements on the frame of the therapy—frame-securing or modifying.
4. Recognition of the currently active *triggering events*, mainly the therapist's impingements on the frame of the therapy.
5. *Linking* the active triggers to the themes to derive the patient's unconscious experience of the triggering event and his or her unconscious responses to it—including, where needed, models of frame rectification.

With this in mind, we can return to the vignette involving Ms Banks presented in chapter 9.

> This patient began her session with the recall of a dream and then engaged in generating narrative guided associating. She produced a pool of themes with both frame allusions [e.g. frame-modifying images such as the pastor's affair and the leakage of confidential information] and power [e.g. the affair, the attack on the pastor, the fractured leg, and the reference to cancer].

All in all, then, in light of the postulated triggering event regarding the pastor's announcement about Dr Tyler's daughter, we can see that Ms Banks made ample use of the communicative defence of disguise or encoding. She thereby produced abundant derivative representations of, and reactions to, the main hypothesized trigger. The result was an impressive amount of encoded meaning in this network of themes, with considerable potential for meaningfully linking with the triggering event to produce decoded insight. In terms of the steps in the decoding process, then, there is to this point almost no signs of communicative resistance.

The main self-indicator (i.e. primarily the patient's impingements on the frame of the therapy) is the patient's thought of joining a committee of which her therapist is a member. This frame-modifying indicator was initially repressed—a sign of a moderate amount of communicative resistance. But once reported, it becomes a target for insight in that the processes of linking and trigger-decoding should reveal the unconscious basis for this intended frame modification. In principle, all intended and acted-upon frame modifications by patients are a response to adaptation-evoking triggers from their therapists, most of them in the form of frame modifications.

The patient's description of this self-indicator has narrative qualities. As all narratives contain trigger-evoked, encoded messages, the patient's plan to have contact with her therapist outside therapy can be taken to represent and encode a prior or different outside contact with and exposure of the therapist.

Finally, this self-indicator is both an action form of resistance against the pursuit of insight within the therapy and serviceable as a potential source of insight. Frame-deviant actions tend to interfere with a patient's communication of encoded themes because the deviation discharges or maladaptively deals with the anxieties evoked by the triggering event to which it is a response. These ground-rule violations are a common response to death-related triggers and to frame deviations by therapists—most of them invoked because of unresolved death anxieties in the therapist.

The next step in the pursuit of trigger-decoded insight involves the search for the most cogent, currently active triggering event(s). With respect to this step in the communicative sequence, Ms Banks completely omitted any manifest representation or recognition of the critical activating triggering event to which she was responding unconsciously—the third-party self-revelation. Even though strong encoded representations were communicated, a direct allusion to the trigger did not materialize, despite considerable effort to find it in the session. It is here that the patient's communicative defences were most intensely active.

Frequently, if the pool of encoded themes is rich, the trigger will be difficult to access. On the other hand, if the trigger is evident, the patient will often have difficulty developing a meaningful pool of themes for trigger-decoding. Without an identified trigger, the encoded themes float in the air without an organizing factor and are lacking in decoded meaning. Linking and deep insight are not possible without an identified trigger.

In all, the absence of all of the components needed for trigger-decoding speaks for the success of a patient's communicative defences and resistances. They have been able to prevent the culmination of the process by which a trigger-decoded, conscious insight is generated.

COMMON COMMUNICATIVE DEFENCES

Given the model of open communicative expression and of the steps from an origination narrative to deep insight, it is possible to create a dictionary of communicative defences. Here, I will sample some of the most common forms taken by these defences.

By definition, a communicative defence is any consciously or unconsciously expressed means by which a patient or therapist interferes with the process of trigger-decoding. It may occur as a resistance in the patient or a counterresistances in the therapist—or both. In all such instances, the obstacles are unconsciously motivated both intrapsychically and interpersonally. Thus, resistances in patients are *always products of the patient/therapist system* and are both internally motivated and empowered by the interventions and unconscious perceptions of the therapist.

There *is a universal dread of the conscious articulation of unconscious experience.* The relevant perceptions and their processing have been relegated to a system that operates without awareness so as to spare the conscious mind—the individual—considerable pain and anxiety. In addition, unconscious experience is very raw, blatantly sexual, violent in its key qualities, often a matter of extremes, and difficult for the conscious mind to tolerate, whether applicable to others or self.

In psychotherapy, where the triggers that evoke the patient's encoded responses are the interventions of the therapist—especially errors in frame management and comment—*both parties* are strongly motivated to prevent these unconscious perceptions from achieving conscious awareness in the patient. The therapist is threatened by realistic perceptions of his or her vulnerabilities and harmful effects on the patient, while the patient wishes to spare the therapist pain and to maintain an idealized image of the therapist. In addition, the patient is under the unconscious influence of needs for harm and punishment because of the influence of deep unconscious guilt. It requires considerable therapeutic work to enable patients (and their therapists) to overcome somewhat these natural tendencies that mitigate against open communication.

The following, stated in terms of patients' typical responses within empowered psychotherapy and relevant to all forms of therapy, are among the most common forms of communicative defence:

1. *A gross and manifest (though unconsciously motivated) opposition to, or failure to engage in, self-processing—the step-by-step pursuit of trigger-decoded insight*. In a word, the rock-bottom defence against the search for deep unconscious meaning and insight consists in standing opposed to the trigger-decoding procedure by knowingly or unknowingly not doing it.
    a. This type of defence takes the form of not accepting or leaving empowered psychotherapy, missing sessions, falling silent, refusing to do a self-processing exercise, stepping out of the defined process into free-associating, intellectualizing, and otherwise not pursuing the steps of the process.
    b. A common form that this defence adopts is the use of clichéd, intellectualized, manifest content self-interpretations that completely bypass the trigger-decoding process. Related to

this defence is the failure by the patient to bring strong frame-related images and power themes into the process—the creation of an unusable pool of themes so that meaningful linking is unfeasible.

c. A patient's dread of consciously experiencing deep unconscious meaning is an interactional phenomenon. It is intensified in the patient when this dread is unconsciously perceived in the therapist on the basis of his or her frame modifications, failures to trigger-decode, and the offer of interventions that interfere with the self-processing pursuit.

d. In terms of individual factors that are likely to evoke this massive form of communicative defence, a history of significant and highly disturbing death-related experiences is most prominent.

e. The finding that patients (and therapists) are not naturally inclined to carry out this process reflects the fixity of the basic mental defences against the pursuit of deep insight.

2. *Poorly configured origination narratives*. A rich, varied, and powerful origination narrative with frame allusions is the basis for a most promising self-processing exercise. Communicative defence is seen when there is a failure to recall a recent dream or, in the absence of a dream, a refusal, claimed inability, or other opposition to making up a story. The origination narrative also may be too bland, or too short or too long, for effective guided associating.

3. *Problems in guided associating*. The guided associations to the origination narrative are the critical source of unconscious meaning. A major type of resistance takes the form of a flight from narrative communication, with very few dream-related guided associated narratives. This is often accompanied by a shift to free-associating and intellectualizing. Another defence is the generation of stories that are thin and flat—weak in power and/or lacking in bridging, encoded frame allusions.

4. *The omission of key self-indicators*. Important self-indicators may be suppressed or overlooked, thereby leaving out significant emotional issues and frame-related behaviours of the patient—usually in the form of frame modifications. The latter may occur

outside the therapy, as in talking to a third party about the therapy or therapist. This is an area about which the therapist knows the least, and therefore he or she will in general be quite uncertain about the level of communicative resistances involved. However, this is also the least critical step in the process, in that trigger-decoding can be completed in the absence of the report of a critical self-indicator.

5. *Trigger identification is erroneous or incomplete.* The patient may fail to make any effort to identify the prevailing triggers. A critical, active trigger may be omitted, or one aspect of a triggering event may be recalled, while a more critical and threatening aspect is ignored. In addition, the patient may use for his or her thematic linking efforts a minor trigger or an old one, while a more critical and pertinent currently active trigger is missed.
   a. Without the conscious identification of the most critical triggers at the moment, effective trigger-decoding and deep insight are not possible.
   b. These omissions are extremely difficult for patients to become aware of because the conscious mind tends inherently to support communicative defences and the obliteration of evocative triggering events—especially when they are death-related. Patients often do not recheck their trigger lists when they have selected a trigger for linking that fails to organize and give deep meaning to their narrative themes. Nor do they tend to turn to their encoded themes as guides for a search for missing triggers. These communicative defences are very common and may be quite difficult to resolve.
6. *Failures to carry out the linking process successfully—the final step in trigger-decoding.* Self-processing culminates in generating trigger-decoded insights and frame-management recommendations that are consciously articulated by linking the encoded themes to their critical, activating triggers. This is perhaps the most difficult part of the process, and it can be beset by resistances that take such forms as:
   a. Simply not engaging in the linking process at all.
   b. Identifying a cogent trigger but failing to find themes

suitable for linking, or using weak and minor themes, to the neglect of those that are more powerful and critical.

c. Engaging in non-linking interpretations that allude to fantasies rather than perceptions, usually restate the obvious, and have a strong intellectual cast.

d. Generating formulations that attempt to relate the themes to triggers, but do so in terms of fantasies about the therapist instead of the more correctly stated decoded unconscious perceptions of his or her actual interventions.

e. Organizing the themes around the patient himself or herself and self-indicators rather than the therapist and his or her triggers. Patients are surprisingly eager to hold themselves instead of their therapists accountable for strongly negative thematic images.

7. *Deficits in the self-monitoring process, which lead to the failure to take corrective action and return an errant self-processing effort to its proper channels.* Some expression of communicative defence and resistances is almost certain to occur in every self-processing exercise. These defences are, however, accessible to recognition by the patient through self-observation, a faculty whose use is required to monitor the self-processing effort and keep it on course.

   a. This requisite creates the opportunity for the invocation *of ancillary communicative defences* in the form of failing to monitor the self-processing effort and in the patient's not realizing that he or she has not fulfilled the requisites of the process. Indeed, failures of self-monitoring are very much the rule, and exceptions are remarkably rare. Inherently, patients tend not to establish a clear picture of this process and do not engage in effective self-observing.

The non-recall and failure consciously to allude to a death-related triggering event in a psychotherapy session is the most common communicative defence humans use when confronted with traumatic experiences that activate death anxiety.

All in all, a detailed list of specific communicative defences would be quite lengthy. As basic modes of self-protection, they are with us at all times, yet in dealing with them, the therapist has the advantage of being able to recognize their presence and subject them, in keeping with therapeutic principles, to direct modification. Finally, we may note that the use of communicative defences is as universal in therapists as it is in patients (see chapter 14).

SOME CONSIDERATIONS OF TECHNIQUE

Technically, the therapist should not, in principle, allude to or introduce a trigger to which a patient has not referred directly. Instead, the therapist should work with the patient to help him or her resolve the communicative and psychological resistances that are the source of this resistance. Communicative studies have shown that resistances are grounded in and inherent to the basic architecture of the emotion-processing mind as activated by psychodynamic factors related to unconscious conflict and anxieties—especially those that are death-related. But given that their identification is far more certain than psychological defences, working first at the communicative level is most productive.

There are two types of communicative resistances. The first involves the mechanics of the trigger-decoding process. They appear as omitted triggers or self-indicators, themes lacking in power and frame allusions, or failures to carry out the linking procedure. These resistances can be recognized directly by the patient, often in response to a request to assess the status of the process at a given point in a session. Once realized, these resistances can be modified through direct efforts of the patient—for example, a missing trigger or type of theme can be provided and used for trigger-decoding.

The second type of resistance is also readily identified, but far more difficult to resolve. It is seen when a patient recognizes that one or more components of the trigger-decoding process are missing, but is unable to provide the missing element. As a rule, this situation arises in the presence of an active and especially disturbing frame-deviant trigger from the therapist. The trigger may be acknowledged, but the themes are flat and without significance, or the themes may be strongly frame-modifying and powerful, but the evocative trigger proves to be elusive. In the latter situation, the themes also reflect the utter danger the patient is experiencing, lest the trigger and its inappropriately seductive and violent meanings emerge as a unit.

The dread here is of the starkly traumatic qualities of the patient's unconscious perception to the therapist in light of the active frame break. Death-related themes are virtually always present, and they reflect the loss for the patient of the therapist who has betrayed and abandoned the patient through the frame violation, and also express the unconsciously experienced violence done to the patient by the frame modification. These powerful themes reveal the motives for the patient's resistances, but interpretations to this effect seldom modify the communicative defences—the dread is far too great. Patient's whose deep unconscious experiences are raw and extreme, and who have a severe history of death-related traumas, tend to be especially resistant in this way.

As for technique, when a patient's attempts at direct recognition of an active trigger related to the existing imagery fail, the therapist's main efforts to alter the communicative resistance should be directed towards the encoded themes in the patient's material. First, the patient is helped to see that the themes reflect in disguised fashion both the nature of the trigger and its most compelling meanings. Then, the frame-related themes are explored for clues to the nature of the adaptation-evoking frame-related intervention.

Secured-frame themes are centred on positive support and wisdom accompanied by threats of entrapment and death—images related to the existential death anxiety activated by therapists' frame-securing interventions. In contrast, deviant-frame interventions evoke themes of frame breaks that also indicate the type of frame modification involved. For example, a fee increase will stimulate themes of stealing or other dishonest and exploitative means of obtaining money. Or a self-revelation by the therapist will produce themes of exposure and nudity.

Like training a detective, the patient is taught to examine the clues available in his or her thematic pool, with the focused goal of translating these clues into a specific frame-related triggering event. Given the patient's needs for defence, this proves to be a slow and arduous therapeutic pursuit.

As a further illustration, consider a narrative image from a male patient of being terrified of being murdered by a criminal if he were to testify against him at a trial. This set of encoded themes suggests that the missing trigger is frame-deviant—the allusion to a crime—and that the patient is terrified of revealing his unconscious perceptions of the trigger to the rule-breaking therapist. Decoding this kind of narrative when a trigger is missing produces a general insight that deals with the dread of carrying forward the trigger-decoding process, but less so with the nature of the missing trigger. The intervention may or may not help to resolve the communicative resistance and enable the patient to recover the missing trigger.

The great frequency with which these defences are used reveals the extent to which the basic human adaptation to highly traumatic triggering events is obliterating rather than actively coping, and the degree to which we have evolved to engage in flight rather than fight in the emotional sphere. Communicative resistances of this kind often are maintained for very long periods of time; their slow modification requires considerable patience in the therapist. Nevertheless, their expression touches on the core of a patient's communicative defences and almost always on how a given patient copes with death anxieties. Thus, their repeated working-over will usually have strong therapeutic effects in the long run. This kind of work is a vital part of what a therapist can offer in the way of a deeply based cure.

This approach to the patient's material truly honours the precept of exploring, analysing, and modifying resistances before contents. Indeed, it shows that contents are not available without the resolution of communicative resistances. In this sense, the communicative approach is faithful to the best of both ego psychology and object relations theory—although it also modifies both of these approaches in its concentration on unconscious perception and experience and the adaptation-oriented process of trigger-decoding.

ACTION/BEHAVIOURAL DEFENCES

In addition to the psychological and communicative types, there is a third group of defences that are products of human thought and reflexive responsiveness, but, rather than being primarily mental, they entail action and behaviour. These actions support all kinds of communicative and psychological defences, not only by being thoughtless in terms of deep meaning, but also by providing avenues of discharge for unconscious needs and contents, which then fail to seek language-based, encoded expression. As we might expect, behavioural defences are very often invoked as part of an obliterating defensive response to death-related triggering events and activated forms of death anxiety.

Ms Banks' lapse, in which she forgot she had a date to see her friend who was recovering from cancer, was an action that was clearly, though quite unconsciously, designed to avoid a situation that was linked to the repressed/denied triggering event that she was processing unconsciously—the announcement of a cancerous illness in her therapist's daughter. The errant behaviour served defensively to avoid a situation that had both conscious and unconscious meanings that were related to this repressed trigger. It was also a way of enacting an occasion of loss that could help discharge an aspect of the patient's unconscious experience of this triggering event so that derivative material would be less likely to appear in her sessions.

Many other common defensive actions are designed to support psychological denial and repression and communicative eradication. In general, they are maladaptive actions that are invoked to deal with death-related issues and anxieties. They include sexual acting-out, especially via frame breaks, manic celebrations, the use of drugs and alcohol, modifications of ground rules and frames, and a wide variety of inappropriate actions that are harmful to self and/or others and are carried out mindlessly and in ways that discharge the conflicts and issues aroused by the unconsciously perceived meanings of triggering events.

Displaced attacks on others and acts of self-harm are typical of these behaviours, which enact representations and defences against the underlying death issues. Indeed, all such behaviours in patients should prompt a search for a death-related triggering event that unconsciously is likely to be the adaptation-evoking stimulus for these costly, maladaptive responses. A great deal of emotionally relevant and inexplicable behaviour serves this kind of defensiveness.

COMMUNICATIVE AND PSYCHOLOGICAL DEFENCES

What, then, is the relationship between the two main classes of mental defence—psychological and communicative? Psychological defences find communicative expression, as seen with repression that leads to communicative lacunae. For their part, communicative defences have psychological effects, as seen with the obliteration of a triggering event that speaks for denial. In general, an analysis of communicative defensiveness illuminates the operations of psychological defences, while the reverse analysis is less certain and less illuminating. Communicative analysis especially facilitates the identification of different forms of both denial and repression, as they operate at different sites in the emotion-processing mind and do so in distinctive fashion. Thus:

1. *Forms of denial*

Psychologically, denial involves the obliteration of a reality event or of apparent aspects of these events. From the communicative perspective, denial is reflected by the absence of a manifest allusion to, or any expressed indication of the awareness of, an event or parts of its meanings. Communicative analysis suggests the existence of three underlying forms or means of denial:

a. *Denial by design—perceptual or deep-unconscious-system denial.* This evolved form of denial has been built into the emotion-processing mind. In response to a traumatic triggering event such as those that are death-related, the human perceptual apparatus may fail consciously to register the event completely, or it may allow some aspects of the event to gain conscious registration and shunt off other evident aspects or meanings to unconscious registration.

The emotion-processing mind appears to have a message-analysing centre attached to its perceptual systems that instantaneously registers and sorts the multiple meanings of an environmental impingement. The centre selectively assigns meanings for transfer to either conscious or unconscious perception; the choice is mutually exclusive. Furthermore, different aspects and meanings of the same triggering event can obtain different assignments.

Thus, perceptual denial is defined as the shunting of all or parts of an environmental impingement to unconscious perception so that the particular meanings are excluded from awareness, often on a permanent basis.

These consciously denied but unconsciously received perceptions do not break directly through into awareness, but as a rule they do emerge in encoded form. Indeed, these denied events or meanings tend not to be recognized consciously when someone else refers to them. Therefore, perceptual denial appears to be a relatively immutable defence.

b. *The denial of repressed but directly retrievable events and meanings.* In this and the following form of denial, this defence operates conjointly with repression. In the first type, conscious perception and registration are followed by strong conscious-system repression that blocks all recollection of the repressed contents. Thus, the repression acts as a form of denial in that the event is removed from conscious experience and obtains no derivative or encoded representation (as it does with conscious-system repression). Intense therapeutic work or the spontaneous modification of this defence by the patient will, however, eventually allow for derivative expression and subsequent direct recall—usually with considerable surprise on the part of the patient. In these cases, a sudden reminder (which should not come from the therapist) may jar loose the obliterated memory from repression.

c. *The complete denial of repressed events and meanings.* Under conditions of extreme trauma, usually death-related, an event and its most disturbing selected meanings may be perceived consciously, but then never again be retrieved into awareness. The sequence here is: conscious perception—storage in the superficial unconscious subsystem of the conscious system—then a shunting over to the deep-unconscious-system memory/storage subsystem from which it is no longer directly retrievable. Thus, an event or meaning that was consciously acknowledged at one time is no longer accessible to awareness, and may for a long while not find derivative expression. Eventually, when activated by a contemporaneous triggering event, these triggers do emerge, but only in encoded narrative images. The shift is from conscious-system repression to denial with deep unconscious storage. As such, this form of denial is also very difficult to undo.

2. *Forms of repression*

Psychological repression also has two main communicative forms:

a. *Conscious-system repression.* This is the generally known form of repression, in that an event or meaning that has registered consciously in the conscious system is shunted into the superficial unconscious memory/storage subsystem, where it expresses itself through thinly disguised, easily decoded images and affects emotional behaviour in self-evident ways. Efforts to bring the repressed contents back into awareness are met with resistance, and recall may not materialize. Eventually, by one means or another, recall does take place, and it does so in direct form—the memory or meaning is retrieved whole cloth, without disguise. *Direct recovery is the hallmark of conscious-system repression.*

b. *Deep-unconscious-system repression.* There are many aspects of unconsciously perceived meanings that are best described as being in a state of deep-unconscious-system repression rather than deep-unconscious-system denial. These meanings are abundantly encoded in a patient's narrative material and are far more readily trigger-decoded than are deeply denied meanings, which are virtually inaccessible for recall and are forever doomed to encoded expression alone. The hallmarks of deeply

> repressed contents are therefore (1) the availability of encoded derivatives of the unconscious experience, and (2) retrievability, though only through trigger-decoding.

In the clinical vignette we have been reviewing, in light of the triggering experience to which Ms Banks presumably was adapting, little degree of certainty attaches to efforts to decide whether denial or repression was the main cause of her not consciously reporting the missing trigger. It cannot be known whether the trigger was not experienced consciously in the first place (which would mean that perceptual denial was at work) or was, instead, experienced consciously and then forgotten or obliterated (the use of conscious-system or deep-unconscious-system repression). Because the trigger is so intense yet does not directly involve the patient, perceptual denial seems unlikely but is possible. Some form of repression, conscious or deep unconscious, seems to explain the non-report better.

An analysis of Ms Banks' communicative defensiveness helps to clarify the nature of Ms Banks' psychological defences. The evident communicative defence is the disguised representation, but conscious non-communication, of a critical adaptation-evoking triggering event. The most likely form of communicative defence in this situation—and it is supported by our post-session knowledge—is that Ms Banks registered this triggering event consciously and subjected it to conscious-system obliteration, with no communicated awareness of the trigger.

As evidenced by her totally absent recollection of the trigger in her session with Dr Tyler, it seems likely that Ms Banks unconsciously shunted the memory of this traumatic announcement from her superficial unconscious subsystem storage/memory system to her deep-unconscious-system storage/memory system. Once embedded in that deep system, the memory of the event would not be retrievable through direct recall, but would find expression via encoded themes/derivatives—which is what we saw from the communicative vantage-point. The trigger, then, could be reclaimed from non-awareness and non-communication only via trigger-decoding. It appears, then, that this vignette is best seen as an example of conscious-system repression that became deep-unconscious-system repression/denial—a defensive sequence that is exceedingly difficult to modify.

SOME FINAL PERSPECTIVES

The relationship between psychological defences and communicative defensiveness is quite important for our understanding of the operations of the emotion-processing mind and for discovering the therapeutic means of modifying maladaptive mental defences. The perspectives gained from this fresh exploration of mental and behavioural defences can be used to provide new insights into the effects of death anxiety on psychotherapy patients, especially with respect to the often mentioned ground rules of therapy—a subject to which we now turn.

CHAPTER THIRTEEN

The patient, the frame, and issues of death

My exploration and clarification of death-related events and death anxiety as they pertain to psychotherapy patients has repeatedly touched on the ground rules of psychotherapy. To complete this discussion, I therefore turn now to a more focused exploration of the interaction between death-related issues and the framework of psychotherapy—the backbone, context, and most powerful influence on the patient's therapeutic experience. The intricacies of the connections between rules, frames, and boundaries and death anxiety are one of the most unappreciated yet critical aspects of our subject.

THE PATIENT AND THE GROUND RULES OF THERAPY

Death anxiety plays a significant role in how patients and therapists deal with the ground rules of therapy, and the vicissitudes of these canons are intimately connected to how each party deals with and adapts to death-related concerns. Both frame-securing and frame-modifying efforts, whether initiated by patient or therapist, are under the influence of strong unconscious motivating sources. Conflicts involving death anxieties play a major role in this respect.

In general, frame-securing efforts speak for adaptive responses to immediate death-related triggers, but they arouse powerful, unconscious existential death anxieties that require resolution. On the other hand, frame modifications tend to reflect maladaptive responses to death-related triggering events and also to evoke unconscious persecutory, predatory death concerns.

In this chapter I shall concentrate on the patient's attitudes towards and requests regarding the structure of the ground rules of therapy (see chapter 15 for a comparable discussion of the therapist).

THE IDEAL OR SECURED FRAME

I shall set the stage for this discussion by reviewing the essential features of the ideal or secured frame. This holding and healing set of ground rules has been *defined over the years by patients' deep unconscious, encoded validating responses to frame-management and frame-related interpretative interventions by therapists*. These observations indicate that the main components of the ideal setting and ground rules are:

1. *The fixed frame:* a professional location and soundproofed office; a set time, frequency, and duration of sessions; and a single fee with responsibility for all scheduled sessions.
2. The obligation that the patient say whatever comes to mind. In the usual therapy this *fundamental rule* is supplemented by the rule of *free association*—that the patient should not direct his or her associations. However, in empowered psychotherapy, this rule is supplemented by a directive to carry out the steps of the process that will take the patient from an initial encoded narrative to a deep unconscious insight. This is the rule of *guided association*.

3. Total privacy and confidentiality.
4. The relative anonymity of the therapist (i.e. no deliberate personal revelations or opinions and intervening entirely on the basis of the patient's material in the session at hand).
5. The therapist's use of neutral interventions, specifically defined as trigger-decoded interpretations and frame-securing efforts carried out on the basis of the patient's encoded directives and validated unconsciously by the patient's responsive encoded narratives.

FRAME ISSUES DURING THERAPY

The status of the ground rules of therapy, including the framework offered by the therapist and that sought by the patient, are, as noted, intimately linked with issues of death anxiety. In general, patients with severe problems with death and related traumas tend to seek modified or compromised frameworks for their therapies. Unconsciously, they are terrified of secured frames because of the overwhelming existential death anxieties they evoke and because they deprive the patient of much-sought pathological and costly defences against trauma-evoked, predatory death anxieties. They prefer and rationalize their insistence on modified frames with alterations in one or more ground rules as a way of defending themselves against these unbearable underlying death-related issues. Similar considerations apply to the type of frame a therapist offers to his or her patients (see chapter 15).

Frame issues arise in psychotherapy in two basic contexts—at the onset of a therapy and during the ongoing treatment experience.

1. *The initial frame*

From the first moment a patient obtains the name of a therapist, the ground rules and framework of therapy are an active and critical force and factor. There are frame-secured and frame-modified ways in which patients obtain the name of a therapist, and similar issues pertain to the question of whether there is a prior relationship between these two parties. For example, a referral by a present or past patient of a therapist is fundamentally frame-deviant (it modifies both the relative anonymity of the therapist and the total privacy and confidentiality due the patient), and the frame modification cannot be rectified unless the therapy is not initiated or is terminated. Similarly, prior contact between patient and therapist, whether in some professional manner or socially, is also an unmodifiable frame modification. On the other hand, referral made by a health-care professional in a formal manner without unneeded revelations about the therapist is frame-securing.

In the initial consultation session, the therapist is obligated to establish as secure a set of ground rules as possible under prevailing conditions. This includes a basic contract and a sound and stable private setting. Here, too, the patient may accept an offered secured frame or request one or another departures from these essential ideals. The manner in which each party deals with the ground rules that establish the basic conditions and framework of a therapy are unconsciously determined by their death-related issues and their preference for adaptive or maladaptive ways of dealing with them.

Although a given patient may accept a secured-frame treatment situation, quite rare is the patient who actively seeks a fully secured set of ground rules. This seems to be a consequence of the prevalence of death-related traumas and unresolved death anxieties that are common to all humans and often especially intense in individuals seeking psychotherapy. Often, the request for treatment follows a loss or other death-related event, so the prospective patient's death anxieties are especially intense. In general, patients who seek secured frames either have an unconscious belief that they can deal with their death-related unconscious experiences or they have been severely damaged by one or more frame-deviant therapists in the past.

Patients with intense secured-frame anxieties resulting from notable death-related traumas will be inclined either to seek out a compromised therapist or to request modifications in the basic ground rules of the therapy. In so doing, they consciously argue for and rationalize the frame modification, even as their deep unconscious systems and encoded narratives speak for secured-frame therapy.

Driven by severe unconscious death anxieties, many of these requests are strongly rationalized consciously. For example, a patient who travels for work may ask for a flexible schedule of therapy sessions, or someone on a limited income may ask for a fee lower than the one asked for by the therapist. In these instances, the therapist must attend to the patient's encoded derivatives and use them to show the patient that they indicate that unconsciously the patient would experience these deviations as both destructive and seductive.

As the material permits, the therapist should also interpret the patient's use of the frame modification to defend against his or her unresolved death anxieties. For example, the patient's associations often reveal that the frame modification is being sought to establish the belief that the patient is an exception to the rules—especially the rule that death follows life. In addition, the insistence on a frame modification is also unconsciously motivated by needs to seek harm and self-punishment from the therapist—often to assuage the deep unconscious guilt connected with the underlying death-related triggering event. Coping with death anxieties with frame modifications within therapy leads to similar efforts at maladaptive coping in the everyday life of the patient—at great cost to self and others.

Despite the usual clarity of the encoded imagery as it pertains to the anticipated trigger of a therapist's possible frame modification, patients with notable death anxieties prove to be very resistant to appreciating consciously these efforts by the therapist. Rationalizations connected with the patient's realistic needs and denial of evident harmful consequences tend to prevail. In dealing with these situations, the therapist is also under pressure from his or her own unresolved death anxieties. These unsettled issues may lead to the acceptance of the patient's rationalizations and the offer of a frame-modified treatment situation. Patient and therapist thereby enter an unconscious misalliance that opposes the deep needs of the patient and the sage recommendations of his or her deep unconscious system, which *always favours the secured frame.* However, in all such cases, regardless of the reality, a deviant framework will serve both patient and therapist as a means of maladaptively denying death anxieties. These arrangements will also interfere with the communication of the encoded derivatives by the patient that are needed to help him or her insightfully to understand and better cope with the death issues that are driving the deviant needs. Both psychological and communicative defences are served in this manner.

In principle, then, frame modifications are conditions that reinforce maladaptive psychological and communicative defences against death anxiety. Frame modifications create conditions under which the patient will, by and large, fail to express encoded narratives or discover the activating triggers that are essential for sound trigger-decoding and therapeutic work.

2. *The ongoing management of the ground rules*

In the course of therapy, a patient may request a temporary or lasting frame change, such as an extra session or one at a different time from the usual, a reduction in the fee, an extended absence, or a report to a third party. The patient may also unilaterally modify the frame by being late or missing a session. In contrast, on rare occasions, a patient will secure an altered frame—for example, by declining a therapist's request to change the time of a particular session.

Here, too, death anxiety is always an underlying issue and factor. The basic responsibility for managing the ground rules of therapy belongs to the therapist—it an aspect of his or her expertise and responsibilities to the patient. But the patient also has obligations and accountability in this regard. A death-related trauma may prompt a patient to modify the frame unilaterally or engage the therapist in doing so. However, the patient generally follows the lead set by the therapist, especially once the therapy has been initiated.

It is critical that the therapist attend to the patient's encoded material when ground-rule issues come to the fore. When a patient secures the frame, positive images will be followed by frightening themes of entrapment and annihilation that are the result of secured-frame holding and anxieties, respectively. Frame modifications will prompt persecutory and other harmful and inappropriately seductive themes that reflect the patient's unconscious perception of the proposed or actual frame break. Here, both interpretation and rectification are called for.

UNCONSCIOUS MOTIVES FOR PATIENTS' FRAME-RELATED ACTIONS

Regardless of the *conscious* need or rationalizations, a patient's frame impingements, whether frame-securing or frame-modifying, are always *unconsciously* motivated by efforts to adapt to death-related triggers and issues. Several factors are of note here.

Securing the frame

Patients are unconsciously motivated to secure the ground rules of their therapies under the following conditions:

1. The patient is in a frame-secured therapy and/or has recently experienced a frame-securing intervention by the therapist. The patient's frame-related behaviours are very much influenced by the therapist's behaviours in this area. Secured-frame therapists tend to engender frame-securing attitudes and behaviours in their patients.
2. Frame-securing by patients often occurs when they have been severely damaged by frame modifications by their present therapist or by one or more previous therapists.
3. Frame-securing by patients may also occur when they are able to appreciate and tolerate without denial their own trigger-decoded frame-securing directives. In some instances the patient is able to do the decoding himself or herself, but more often the therapist plays the major role in these efforts.

In grim testimony to the great difficulties we all have in adapting to death anxiety, communicative studies indicate that while patients consistently encode their need and preferences for secured frames, actual frame-securing efforts by patients are quite rare. However, frame-modifying derivatives are virtually non-existent, yet conscious frame-modifying efforts are extremely common.

Most importantly, a therapist needs to appreciate the adaptive value of a patient's frame-securing actions—attributes that will be reflected in the patient's encoded narratives. Both the affirming positive encoded images and the subsequent secured-frame entrapment and annihilatory images related to existential death anxieties must be understood and interpreted for what they are. There is no more powerful moment in psychotherapy than one that is frame-securing. This event possesses enormous holding and healing qualities, yet it generates some of the most fearsome death anxieties experienced by patients and therapists alike. A full appreciation of the therapeutic value of frame-secured therapies and frame-securing moments in deviant treatments enables therapists to offer the best possible therapy experience to their patients.

Modifying the frame

Frame modifications by patients are, virtually without exception, behavioural efforts to cope maladaptively with trigger-evoked death anxieties in ways that will support both denial-based psychological defences and communicative forms of obliteration that prevent access to deep unconscious experience. Many of these efforts to alter secured ground rules are activated by death-related triggers within therapy or outside it. But even those changes that are realistically necessary for the continuation of a therapy, such as a permanent shift in the time of a session because of a job change, will be appropriated by patients to support their maladaptive coping responses to death anxiety.

Frame modifications by patients are sought unconsciously to defend maladaptively against activated death anxieties. They tend to be highly varied and often ingeniously rationalized, and they can tax the therapist's resourcefulness to recognize and respond appropriately through trigger-decoded interpretations and frame-sustaining interventions. Because they always touch on the therapist's own death anxieties and defences, frame-modifying pressures from patients often lead therapists to deviate, despite directives in the patient's derivative material to do otherwise.

The following are among the most common frame modifications sought by patients:

1. With regard to the fixed frame, there may be requests for fee reductions, extra sessions, contact with the therapist outside the office, and increasing or decreasing the frequency of the sessions.
2. With respect to the more variable aspects of the ground rules, instead of saying whatever comes to mind, the patient may elect to conceal material or fail to report thoughts and feelings because they are deemed trivial, inadvertent, or too difficult to talk about. In empowered psychotherapy, the patient may depart from the defined procedures and insist on free-associating rather than engaging in guided associating, or may fail to carry out the various steps of the process.
3. A patient may attempt to alter the privacy and confidentiality of his or her therapy by introducing or trying to introduce third parties. For example, family, friends, health-related professionals, or others may be brought into the treatment situation in a variety of ways. The therapist may be asked to release information to a third party, or the patient may discuss the therapy with an outside figure.
4. Patients may also try to get their therapists to modify their relative anonymity by pursuing personal information about their therapists—directly from the therapist or from third parties. In addition, patients may seek their therapists' personal views and ideas. These efforts may involve direct pressures or be conveyed indirectly through provocative comments by the patient.
5. Similar efforts are made by patients to modify therapists' neutrality through requests for non-interpretative interventions, such as advice, direct support, and the like.
6. A most malignant and generally unacknowledged frame modification involves patients' offers to refer friends, relatives, and acquaintances to their therapists either during or after treat-

ment. This frame deviation modifies patients' total confidentiality and privacy and often leads to additional frame breaks.

Because patient referrals are an excellent example of frame alterations that have no evident connection to death anxiety, a brief clinical excerpt will show how exploration reveals a deep unconscious and maladaptive tie to death issues.

Vignette: a patient referral

Mr Kelly, a married man in his forties who was disturbed by problems in his marriage and some overuse of alcohol, entered therapy with Mr Fish, a social-work therapist who was trained in a general psychodynamic approach to therapy. In a session two years into his therapy, the patient asked the therapist whether he had time to see a friend, Mrs Flowers, whose brother had recently died in a car accident. Mr Fish said he would be glad to see her in consultation. Mr Kelly thanked him and added that she needed a great therapist like Mr Fish because she had been very close to her brother.

The patient went on to say that for some reason he was thinking now of a weird story he had read in the newspaper about a head of a religious sect who was accused of having sex with his followers, men and women alike. The man was exposed by a young woman who had been brought into the sect by one of its members, because the religious leader had immediately tried to seduce her. He had become very forceful with his affections, but the woman held him off and reported him to the police. The police discovered that earlier one of the women the leader had tried to seduce had committed suicide. Many members quit the group when the scandal came to light. Mr Kelly was of the opinion that the man must have been an insatiable maniac and should be put in jail for the rest of his life. No one should need so many lovers, let alone from both sexes.

Mr Kelly next said that he should not be worrying about the problems of other men, as he had enough of his own. He was not getting along well with his wife again—she meant well but

> often did stupid things. She had been caught lifting money from the cash box where she worked—she would do almost anything for a bit of extra cash. The whole thing was such a mess, and he felt an alcoholic binge coming on.
>
> Mr Fish eventually interpreted this material as a reflection of Mr Kelly's view of his father, who had had several affairs, as his children had discovered. The therapist also suggested that the story might well reflect a wish to have sex with him, in the transference, and to be assaulted sexually as a punishment for his drinking. His view of his mother seemed to be reflected in his feelings towards his wife, the therapist added; it was time he separated his image of his wife from that of his mother.

At this point, the narrative material can be trigger-decoded in light of its immediate triggering event. Mr Fish had modified the therapy frame by accepting a patient referral. This act alters the one-to-one privacy and confidentiality of this therapy and also compromises the therapist's relative anonymity. The patient's request and the frame break itself followed two frame modifications that Mr Fish had invoked three weeks earlier—a unilateral decision to increase Mr Kelly's fee and a change that week in the time and day of their session.

Outside the therapy, Mr Kelly's boss at work had died suddenly of a brain haemorrhage some two weeks before the session excerpted above. The patient had been so upset that he had requested and was seen for an extra session, during which his manifest thoughts and feelings about the loss were worked over, but no effort was made to trigger-decode his narratives, which were replete with power and deviant-frame allusions triggered by holding the deviant session.

On this basis, Mr Kelly's offer and Mr Fish's acceptance of the referral may be viewed as:

1. An action designed to support his denial of and defensive non-communication about the psychological harm that his therapist had caused by his previous frame deviations and other errant interventions. The prior deviations are characterized in these narratives as malevolently seductive, murderous, dishonest,

and addictive. The patient referral helps the patient to avoid direct exploration of these past frame changes and serves to deny the patient's unconscious perceptions of the therapist's failings—consciously, he is admired and thought of highly enough to deserve a referral.

2. Mr Fish's compliance is a behavioural support for Mr Kelly's denial of his *unconscious perceptions* of unresolved death anxieties in his therapist—a view that is based on Mr Fish's recent frame modifications. With few exceptions, therapists who initiate alterations in the ground rules do so under personal pressure from unresolved death-related traumas, often of recent origin.
   a. The request to refer a patient to Mr Fish is also an unconscious effort to allay the therapist's death anxieties through the creation of a situation in which loss is minimized or negated—the loss of one patient through any means is compensated for by the presence of the other patient.
3. The request is also a maladaptive effort to cope with the death of Mr Kelly's boss through denial and undoing. In this case, the "birth" of a new patient undoes the loss of his boss. Similarly, the new patient will serve to undo the unconsciously imagined loss recently suffered by the therapist.
   a. This maladaptive means of trying to cope with the loss of the boss follows the frame-modifying model of coping offered by Mr Fish through his earlier deviations. Frame-modifying therapists unconsciously encourage the use of frame deviations by their patients.
4. Finally, this conjoint violation of the ground rules of therapy unconsciously and delusionally supports the fantasy that the patient and the consenting therapist are exceptions to the existential rule that death follows life. In this way, death anxiety is assuaged, but further maladaptive expressions of this denial mechanism are then needed to support this defence—with disastrous consequences for all concerned.

To derive the specific unconscious meanings of these encoded narratives, we may begin with the immediate triggering event and decode the themes accordingly. Themes link to their trigger as adaptive unconscious perceptions of and reactions to the therapist in light of his or her most immediate frame modification. The most compelling trigger at the moment is the therapist's decision to see the referred patient. Extracting the story's themes and linking them to the triggering event, Mr Kelly appears to have unconsciously experienced this decision as a seductive and promiscuous act, a betrayal of himself, and a rape of the referred patient. To him, the therapist's decision is a greedy, exploitative act. This is a trying decoding effort in that it is difficult for therapists to accept these unconscious assessments of their manifestly well-intended but defensive and hurtful frame-deviant interventions.

The suicide of a sect member introduces the theme of death. This image evidently reflects the patient's unconscious despair over the therapist's decision. It is also an attempt to let the therapist know that his decision is destructive to his patient and himself. Finally, it is based on some unknown-to-the-patient source of death anxiety within Mr Fish. Patients typically and correctly unconsciously sense that death anxieties lie behind therapists' needs to modify treatment frames. (In this case, unknown to Mr Kelly, Mr Fish's had suffered a significant death in his family.)

The reaction of the patient to this trigger also includes wishes to punish the therapist (put him in jail) and a corrective or model of rectification: don't be so greedy; don't accept this referral. The stories also indicate that if Mr Fish does see Mrs Flowers, the patient will be inclined unconsciously to rectify the deviation by quitting the therapy—leave the corrupt leader/therapist. However, given that his deep unconscious wisdom is unavailable for conscious adaptive decisions, the patient's leaving therapy is unlikely. Instead, Mr Kelly will probably remain in this therapy and unconsciously exploit his therapist's deviation to shore up his own frame-deviant maladaptive defences.

> Mrs Flowers did call and was seen by Mr Fish. In addition to talking about the death of her brother, she reported a dream in which *a friend takes her to a seance at which the medium contacts her brother and brings him back to life.* The dream brought to mind a story on television about a medium who fraudulently rigged a seeming return to life of a child lost by a woman. The woman

was led to believe that her son was really in the room with her, telling her what to do with her savings. The scheme was an attempt to extort money from the woman, who went crazy when the scam was exposed.

The triggering event for Mrs Flowers' encoded narratives is Mr Fish's agreeing to see her as a patient referred by another patient. While the trigger is not referred to directly by the patient, it is strongly represented in encoded fashion in the dream image of the woman who takes the patient to see a medium. The unconscious perception of the therapist in light of this deviant intervention is that of a charlatan interested in defrauding her of her money by doing something that creates the illusion of bringing the dead back to life. The patient wants to share this illusion with her therapist, but realizing the truth of the situation and the meanings inherent in the therapist's agreeing to see her would drive her crazy. This is a rather grim image in the face of the therapist's well-meaning conscious intentions to be helpful even as unconsciously he is actually being quite harmful.

There will be real consequences as a result of the patient's unconscious experience of the therapist's frame-deviant session with her. For example, Mrs Flowers will be inclined to displace her experience of being exploited onto friends and relatives in her daily life, and she might well develop an iatrogenic (therapist-caused) paranoid syndrome. She might also realize consciously, via trigger-decoding, her deep unconscious impression that she was being exploited by Mr Fish for his financial gain and, as in her story, decompensate with a serious mental breakdown.

Consciously, Mr Kelly thanked Mr Fish for agreeing to see Mrs Flowers, and for her part, she came willingly and without complaint to her consultation session. In each case, their deep unconscious perceptions and wisdom appeared to be highly critical of the therapist but did not affect their adaptive behaviours regarding the therapy situation.

Both patients did, however, suffer from a number of displaced symptoms. For example, in a session after Mr Fish saw Mrs Flowers, Mr Kelly described how he had incorrectly accused a fellow worker of fraud. He had also fought with his wife because she wanted to adopt a child, even though he was inclined to favour the idea. In her second session, Mrs Flowers reported that she had mistakenly accused her husband of infidelity, and she had argued with her sister over money because she had incorrectly thought that her sister was trying to steal from her.

* * *

There is, then, evidence of strong unconscious motives in both of these patients and their therapist to find frame-modifying ways of maladaptively trying to resolve active death issues and anxieties. The simultaneous emergence of these pathological needs in all three individuals created a three-party misalliance designed magically and delusionally to deny loss and death. The frame modification was a way of trying to live out the unconscious delusional belief that death can be undone and loss prevented—that death can be defeated. A therapy situation with three participants is almost death proof—if any one person dies, there will still be two survivors who go on.

Introducing Mrs Flowers into his therapy situation and her acceptance of a therapist who was seeing her friend were maladaptive ways of unconsciously trying to undo the death of Mr Kelly's boss and Mrs Flowers brother—and the loss of Mr Fish's family member as well.

Beyond these specific denial-based fantasies, which are supported by the frame modification, the deviation was invoked to enable both patients to avoid devastating encoded derivatives related to these two death experiences—a defensiveness that Mr Fish, given his own recent loss, unconsciously welcomed and supported. There is, in addition, on all sides a defiance of the secured frame and the reassurance that with the rules of therapy broken, the rules that the dead stay dead and that death follows life can also be broken. These are the kinds of delusional unconscious beliefs and defensive needs that motivate and are supported by these types of frame breaks.

Frame-altering requests and actions have as one unconscious source the death anxieties of the patient. This means that the therapist's response will reinforce or establish the patient's means of adapting to these anxieties, including their adaptive and maladaptive features. The ideal therapeutic response is both interpretative and frame-securing, based on the encoded narrative messages and directives in the patient's material. Failure to interpret and/or sustain the secured frame will support deviant and uninsightful maladaptive responses to death anxiety by the patient and will promote symptom formation, acting out, and other harmful actions directed towards self and other.

Frame alterations initiated by patients are also always unconsciously motivated psychodynamically. They can express a variety of needs, impulses, and defences such as seducing, harming, merging with or escaping from the therapist, and undermining the therapy. They are action/behavioural forms of defence that tend to bypass encoded meaning and trigger-decoded insight, and they are an action/frame-altering means of dealing with death anxiety by providing denial-based unconscious illusions and delusions that death is defeated by the power of the patient to modify rules and boundaries. The key here is the unconscious belief that the violation of any ground rule is equivalent to having the power to defy the existential rule that death follows life.

These unconscious fantasies and beliefs underlie every frame break. This means, then, that illusory, denial-based, communication-destroying defences against death anxiety are basic to every frame modification. In addition, many frame alterations allow for a fantasied merger with the therapist and the undoing of separateness from him or her, as seen with having an extra session, gaining personal information about the therapist, and having contact with him or her outside therapy. The undoing of loss is equivalent to undoing the threat of death.

SOURCES OF PATIENTS' DEVIATIONS

To summarize, patients' frame modifications stem from the following sources:

1. *A frame modification by the therapist.* Frame modification by therapists begets frame modifications by their patients. The therapist's frame breaks tend to create vicious circles of denial-

based, communication-interfering, frame-modifying defences against death anxiety that are enacted by both parties in these situations.

Given that these maladaptive responses to death-related triggering events are programmed into the evolved design of the emotion-processing mind and reinforced by psychodynamic factors, the surrender of these costly defences is a critical aspect of deep cure. Achieving this goal, then, requires both behavioural rectification by forgoing frame deviations, accepting secured frames, and developing deep insight into the activated underlying conflicts, anxieties, and issues. The shift from a frame-deviating mode to one that is frame-securing creates powerful therapeutic interludes that often require long periods of time to effect but yield even longer-lasting rewards.

2. *The securing of the frame by the therapist.* In general, frame-securing by therapists evokes frame-securing by patients. The exceptions to this pattern come from patients suffering from the syndrome of excessive death anxiety caused by over-intense exposure to death-related problems (see below). While all patients experience and have an ideal opportunity to work through their existential death anxieties under frame-securing conditions, these extremely death-sensitive patients will affirm the positive effects of a frame-securing intervention but then react with excessive death anxiety and terrible images of entrapment and annihilation. Survivor guilt, needs for punishment, and the overwhelming horrors and helplessness caused by inordinately traumatic death experiences play a role in these terrified reactions to the secured frame and can therefore unconsciously motivate patients to engage in frame-modifying responses to therapists' frame-sustaining interventions.

3. *A death-related traumatic triggering event connected with the therapist and the therapy.* All death-related experiences involving a therapist will strongly activate his or her patients' death anxieties. Common examples include the patients' knowledge of the death of another patient of the therapist or of an illness in the therapist or a member of his or her family. A frequent aspect of the maladaptive response to these triggering events is one or more death-denying frame deviations enacted or requested by

the patient, typically modelled on one or more frame modifications by the therapist, who is inclined to deal with his or her own death anxieties in a frame-deviant manner.

4. *A death-related trauma/trigger in the private life of the patient.* The anxieties aroused by death-related personal traumas often lead patients in therapy to request or unilaterally invoke frame modifications in their therapies—for example, a request for an additional session or for an increase in the frequency of sessions.

Whatever the initiating source of a patient-evoked frame alteration, the frame break is once again an action in the service of denying death anxiety and disrupting the conscious and unconscious communication of death-related imagery. It is to be stressed, then, that these responses are always maladaptive and cause harm for all concerned—within therapy and outside it. The ideal therapeutic response to these interludes once again entails being able to hold the frame and to gain deep insight into the activated unconscious death-related issues so as to discover more effective and less costly ways of coping with the activated death-related conflicts and anxieties.

THE SYNDROME OF EXCESSIVE DEATH ANXIETY

Many patients who seek psychotherapy are suffering from one or another form of a critical and not uncommon death-related pathological syndrome—*the syndrome of excessive death anxiety caused by over-intense exposure to death-related traumas.* This syndrome is characterized by extreme defensiveness, psychologically and communicatively, directed against death-related conscious and unconscious expressions and concerns. This is especially true of efforts to work over the conscious and unconscious ramifications of the patient's early-life traumas and later death-related triggering events—the mental resistance against such work is massive. In addition, these patients are extremely secured-frame-anxious and sensitive.

The following are the main features of this syndrome:

1. A history of one or more devastatingly traumatic death-related experiences. This may involve, for example, the loss of a parent in early childhood or the loss of a loved one in a violent manner, such as through an accident, suicide, or murder. Or it may entail a personal near-death experience or the personal involvement in the death of someone else, as in a car crash in which the patient was the driver, or being a party to an abortion. The personal experience of severe illness, injury, disability, or impending death may also be the evocative issue.
2. Usually, these patients will speak directly though sparingly of these incidents, but their conscious working-over of these experiences is flat, isolated, affectless, intellectualized, distant, and constricted. Use is made of considerable conscious-system denial, repression, and avoidance.
3. The development of seemingly immutable psychological and communicative defences against the expression of encoded narrative derivatives related to traumatic triggering events.
4. Behaviourally, the lives of these patients are marked with suffering and difficulties that seem to be matters of bad luck and external happenstance, but actually they are unconsciously motivated and arranged because of the unconscious rage, guilt, and needs for self-punishment and self-harm evoked by these events.
5. The secured-frame anxieties in these patients are excessive and unconsciously near-delusional in that they believe that they will be destroyed or perish within the confines of such a frame. This includes a sense that the encoded material that would emerge under secured-frame conditions would be psychologically unbearable and overwhelming. For these reasons, these patients usually seek out deviant-frame therapies and therapists, and they often flee secured-frame therapists even as they unconsciously validate their frame-securing interventions.
6. These patients require sensitive efforts by their therapists to find a safe course between the Scylla of offering them the harmful frame modifications they seek and the Charybdis of secur-

ing the frame of their therapies and frightening them to the point where they flee treatment. These patients are sometimes called the damned in that they seem damned to eternal conflict—they are also *damned* difficult to treat.

DEATH AND THE PATIENT

To summarize, death becomes an active issue for patients in psychotherapy in the following ways:

1. when there is a history of a severe death-related trauma;
2. when a death-related trauma occurs in the course of a therapy;
3. when the ground rules or frame of therapy is either secured or modified—this being the main non-death event to evoke death anxieties;
4. when a patient becomes suicidal or homicidal;
5. when a patient or therapist is elderly, seriously ill, injured, or dying.

In many of these situations, the patient's dread of meaning, especially unconscious meaning, and of secured frames, is quite extreme. Should the therapist modify the frame or fail to interpret death-related derivatives in light of active triggers, the patient will unconsciously perceive the therapist as suffering from severe death anxieties of his or her own—perceptions that increase the patient's own anxieties in this area.

Technically, a patient who suffers a loss or threat of loss through death will be inclined to seek frame-deviant forms of therapy or to request frame modifications in an existing therapy. Therapists should be on the alert for these frame-altering efforts and should not create a misalliance by agreeing to them, but should instead properly manage and interpret these efforts based on the patient's encoded imagery.

Death may arise in the therapy in the form of a suicidal or homicidal patient, or a seriously ill or dying patient. These situations are extremely trying for the psychotherapist who correctly understands that securing frames is health-promoting, and modifying them is, in general, regression-promoting.

In cases where suicidal or homicidal impulse are at issue, there is a delicate balance: on the one hand, holding the frame secured assists the patient significantly in sustaining his or her controls and refraining from violence. On the other hand, there may be emergency calls for help via added sessions that must be carefully assessed so that disaster is avoided. Only on *extremely rare occasions* should an emergency session be granted to the patient; it will be consciously appreciated but unconsciously criticized and seen as deviantly gratifying, seductive, and entrapping.

It is, however, critical to realize that these emergencies arise in one of several contexts, and some are the responsibility of the therapist. Here, too, prior frame deviations by the therapist play an important role. A therapist who has been frame-securing is not likely to receive a frame-deviating request from a patient and is usually spared the dilemma of deciding how to deal with a damned-if-you-do/damned-if-you-don't frame-altering entreaty. When the choice is made to opt for due caution by seeing the patient in an emergency session, the patient's unconscious perceptions of the deviant intervention must be interpreted as material becomes available.

The patient who is seriously ill or dying poses another problem for the therapist. Patients who are in the throes of death suffer from extremes of death anxiety. They dread both the secured frames with which they are struggling as their life nears an end and the unconscious meanings that death poses for them. Their frame-breaking and denial needs are enormous.

Many of these patients will simply not stay with a therapist who attempts to secure the ground rules of their therapy and endeavours to trigger-decode their unconscious responses to activated triggers related to the therapist's interpretations and frame-securing efforts and, secondarily, the patient's own illness. However, a therapist who appreciates secured frames and the value of trigger-decoding unconscious meanings and who then fails to sustain the frame or interactionally interpret the patient's encoded imagery is unconsciously perceived by these patients as terrified of death and as useless to them.

Dealing with these difficult situations is a communicative dilemma in need of creative solutions. As our knowledge now stands, it seems best for a therapist to maintain a trigger-decoding, frame-securing position in the hope that it will give strength to the patient, and to consider frame modifications and avoiding interpretative interventions only when the patient seems overwhelmed or the continuation of the therapy is threatened (see chapter 16).

Finally, a word about patients who are in their later years—those over 50 or 60 or so. These patients are at all times actively coping with death anxieties. Whatever issues confront them, whether in therapy or otherwise, there will be a strong link to death-related triggers and concerns. No segment of therapeutic work is complete with these patient unless the death aspect is brought to the fore. Most certainly, it will be reflected in the patient's encoded material as its themes link up with active triggers. The interpretation of this material in the context of a secured frame is a most therapeutic experience for these patients as they deal with the falling shadows of their lives.

PART THREE

Death issues and the therapist

CHAPTER FOURTEEN

Death anxiety and the psychotherapist

Every aspect of the lives of psychotherapists, both personal and professional, is deeply affected by death anxieties and death-related issues. These effects extend to their life work and influence their choice of psychotherapy as a profession, the particular theory and approach they select as their basis for doing therapy, their preferences regarding the kind of framework and the setting they offer to their patients, and the specific interventions they make on a daily basis.

Each patient whom a psychotherapist treats brings to therapy a specific death-related history and works over, consciously and unconsciously, a variety of death-related experiences as his or her therapy unfolds. All of these factors, in both therapist and patient, will deeply affect a therapist's interventions and behaviours vis-à-vis the patient in question. Death-related issues are a critical component of every treatment situation, and they greatly influence the spiralling, circular interaction between patient and therapist. The effects of death-related traumas spread from a therapist's everyday life into his or her work with patients, much as the effects also spread from the clinical work into the therapist's everyday life—death knows no boundaries.

THE THERAPIST'S CHOICE OF PROFESSION

Communicative explorations give both deeper meaning and irony to the old joke, common in the days of predominantly medical psychoanalysis, that a psychoanalyst is a doctor who cannot stand the sight of blood (i.e. death). The relative absence of psychoanalytic writings on the subject of death and the inclinations of analysts towards the use of frame-modifying defences against death anxiety strongly suggest the truth of this statement.

Most medical specialists deal with large numbers of patients who are seriously ill physically. This is far less the case for psychotherapists, who, by and large, treat physically healthy or minimally to moderately ill patients. Their patients also tend to be at an age where death is seldom a pressing concern. Psychotherapy is concentrated on the healing process, and little time is spent seeking diagnoses that often reflect considerable skill but involve fatal diseases.

However, as this book shows, paradoxically, the escape from death as a physical event brings therapists into a psychotherapy situation in which the psychological factors and emotional experiences of death are an ever-present and powerful manifest or latent issue. This insight bears another testimony to death's inescapable presence in all types of healing endeavours.

* * *

In terms of psychoanalytic theory, Freud's position on death anxiety as distinct from a death instinct seems to stand without serious challenge to the present. Articulated in three of his late-life revolutionary works—"Beyond the Pleasure Principle" (Freud, 1920a), *The Ego and the Id* (Freud, 1923b), and *Inhibitions, Symptoms and Anxiety* (Freud, 1926d [1925])— he primarily posited a human death instinct that spoke for a wish to die. In this way, Freud essentially turned the fear of death into a deep wish that served to deny the existence of death anxiety. He also specifically denied a psychodynamic importance to death anxiety by reducing it to the loss of the love of the superego on the one hand, and castration anxiety on the other. Thus, in taking issue with his follower, Stekel, Freud wrote:

> The high-sounding phrase, "every fear is ultimately the fear of death" has hardly any meaning, and at any rate cannot be justified . . . for death is an abstract concept with a negative content for which no unconscious correlative can be found. [Freud, 1923b, pp. 57–58]

In this passage and elsewhere, Freud elaborated on his refutation of death anxiety as a motivating force and unconscious factor in emotional dysfunctions. He offered death little place in his analytic work with patients, even though it played a notable but personally unacknowledged role in his early life and self-analysis.

There are recent indications, however, that these denial-based trends are beginning to change. The attention being paid to dying patients and the growing number of individuals suffering from syndromes likes AIDS confront therapists more strongly than ever with death-related issues, and an elaborate literature is being developed on existential issues and post-traumatic stress disorders. However, the deep unconscious aspects of death-related issues and the many extended effects that death and death anxiety have on humans have not been effectively addressed in these writings, which are largely confined to manifest ideas about, and responses to, these problems.

DEATH ISSUES AND MODES OF THERAPY

There are now some 300 forms of psychotherapy, which can be categorized roughly into some dozen or so major groups. While I will not attempt an exhaustive listing, I will offer a sampling that helps to clarify how death-related issues affect the choice of a therapist's mode of therapy and its theoretical support system.

Therapies vary from those that tend to obliterate automatically any semblance of death-related communications and issues as much as possible to those that focus on conscious responses to death issues, and, finally, those that attempt to allow patients the expression of representations of the intense *unconscious* experiences activated by death-connected events and try to interpret the resultant material in sound fashion.

The key factors in defining the extent to which a therapy is open to and effective in dealing with death-related issues are:

1. *The nature of the ground rules and frame sanctioned and advised by the particular approach.* Theories that are lax about frame management and allow for many frame modifications tend to support and foster the patient's use of obliterating psychological and communicative defences against death anxiety. On the other hand, the more secure-frame-oriented a clinical practice and theory is, the more likely it is that deep unconscious responses to death issues will be available for exploration and interpretation.
2. *The interpretative approach sanctioned by a given theory.* Manifest-content approaches simply cannot access deep unconscious experience and meaning as they pertain to death-related events. Only approaches that make use of trigger-decoding can do so.

In general, frame-sensitive approaches to psychotherapy also tend to be sensitive to encoded derivatives and to allow for a working-through of deep unconscious responses to death-related traumas—past and present.

THE CHOICE OF THEORY AND MODE OF THERAPY

Among the many factors that influence a therapist's selection of a psychotherapy modality and theory, the status of his or her death anxiety constellation is of considerable importance. The more severe a therapist's death-related historical profile and deep unconscious death anxieties, the greater the likelihood that he or she will decide for an obliterating, defensive form of therapy. A death-sensitive therapist is unconsciously unable to tolerate patients' deep unconscious experiences of death-related triggering events and will offer a treatment modality where the possibility of relevant encoded expressions of these issues is minimized. Death-related formulations will be all but excluded.

These attitudes are influenced by a therapist's own life experiences as well as his or her personal therapy experience. The latter includes the conscious and unconscious attitudes on death-related issues of his or her psychotherapist. A therapist's original choice of a therapist is also affected by his or her death-related history, death anxieties, and active death-related issues.

By virtue of mental design and psychodynamic factors, nonprofessional patients select therapists largely for unconscious defensive reasons. Therapists also tend to select therapists because of similar needs—frame modifications are very common in their psychotherapy situations. Both the therapist–patient's own needs and what he or she senses about how a prospective therapist deals with his or her own death anxieties play a role in these choices. A maladaptive—that is, denying—defensive frame-modifying misalliance between therapist–patients and their therapists is a not uncommon occurrence—with considerable consequences for the future work of the fledgling therapist.

These problems are especially severe for therapists suffering from the syndrome of excessive death anxiety caused by overintense exposure to death-related traumas. These therapists often are simply incapable, without extended communicative psychotherapy (which they dread to experience), of sustaining and working effectively within a secured frame and with death-related derivatives from patients. Perhaps the clearest example of this kind of situation is seen with Holocaust survivors whose death-related traumas are among the most terrible humans have suffered. Many of these individuals have fashioned very popular, elaborate death-denying theories of psychotherapy as a means of denying and avoiding their own death-related issues and trying in some desperate way to manage the overbearing death anxieties that threaten from within to erupt at any moment.

Aside from individual and group therapies that are designed specifically to work over a patient's conscious (but not deep unconscious) responses to death-related traumas (as in groups for

AIDS patients), psychotherapies and their underlying theoretical constructs fall roughly into three groups in this respect.

1. *Maximally obliterating*

These are modes of therapy that (1) allow for great latitude in departures from the ideal secured frame; (2) sanction extensive non-interpretative interventions by the psychotherapist, including directives, questioning, advice-giving, selecting non-death topics for discussion, and the like; (3) find ways to avoid or minimize death as an issue; and (4) make no attempt to process or interpret unconscious meanings but confine the therapist's work to realistic issues and manifest contents.

a. Common examples include family and couple therapies, group therapies, outreach forms of therapy with case management and home visits, cognitive therapies, most forms of inpatient (hospital-based) therapy, and most residential treatment programmes.

b. As far as the secured frame is concerned, these therapies are founded on a theoretical structure that fails to recognize and understand the critical role in therapy played by the conditions of treatment. Sanctioned deviations occur in abundance and may include, for example, limited physical contact between patient and therapist; seeing more than one patient from a given family at a time; looseness regarding the locale of the sessions (home–office arrangements abound) and the time that sessions are held; videotaping sessions and other violations of the patient's right to, and need for, privacy and total confidentiality; and social contacts between patients and therapists during treatment and especially after it has been completed.

c. In terms of the accessibility of death-related material, these treatment modes are unwittingly designed to reduce greatly themes that are consciously and unconsciously connected with death-related issues. Only occasionally will a death or serious illness that affects the patient be allowed to find any measure of conscious exploration. However, the results of these discussions, in which the therapist is likely to be very active and imposing, tend to be clichéd, superficial, self-evident, and with little or no dynamic sense; no effort is made to deal with encoded meanings and deep unconscious experience.

These therapists fail to appreciate that the unconscious aspects of death issues can be dealt with only when activated by death-related triggering events, including both frame-securing and frame-modifying interventions. It is the unconscious meanings in encoded themes that embody a patient's most dreaded perceptions and experiences of these triggers and of the therapist who generates them.

d. These treatment modalities offer both patients and therapists significant obliterating defences against the expression and exploration of death-related issues. The poorly structured ground rules of these therapy situations and the laxness with which the frame is managed by the therapist create conditions of deep unconscious mistrust of the therapist, which reduces this work to a minimum. Frame deviations tend to discharge death anxieties in costly ways that reduce the communication of encoded messages related to these issues. While they produce unconscious predatory perceptions and death anxieties, they also defend the patient and therapist from far more dreaded forms of existential death anxiety.

These non-interpreting, frame-deviant therapists are unconsciously viewed by their patients as fearful of death and as suffering from significant amounts of unresolved death anxiety—unconscious perceptions that intensify the patient's own obliterating defences in this area. Patients unconsciously do a great deal to protect their therapists from being overwhelmed by their own—and their therapist's—death anxieties, and avoidance is the key to these unwitting protective measures.

The excessive verbal activities employed by these therapists, which are supported and rationalized by their underlying theories, make it all but impossible for a patient to narrate and convey encoded expressions, because so much of the session is occupied with questions, intellectualizations, and explanatory non-narrative answers. And should one of these patients happen to embark on a storied communication, the therapist will almost always interrupt the narrative with a diverting question or a comment that cuts off the tale being told—and its encoded death-related images and unconscious meanings.

It is to be expected that therapists who suffer from excessive unresolved death anxieties will be drawn to therapy forms of this type so that they can be spared the activation of their own death issues.

2. *Moderately obliterating*

These are treatment modalities that (1) at times maintain a semblance of a secured frame, though usually with some modifications in the ground rules that are built into the basic therapy contract or that arise in the course of the therapy; (2) allow for a wide range of non-interpretative interventions, which are, however, used only to a moderate extent; and (3) make some effort, however superficial, constricted, and often erroneous, to explore and interpret unconscious experience and meaning as they pertain to death issues.

a. Examples of this type of therapy include most forms of psychoanalytic treatment and insight-oriented psychotherapies.

b. The approach to the ground rules by these therapists is highly varied, ranging from those who adhere to most of the ideal unconsciously validated ground rules most of the time to those who are far more lax in this respect.

c. Frame modifications are abundant in virtually all so-called training analyses; they set an unrecognized frame-deviant, death-denying tone for the candidate's life and therapeutic work. These frame-related effects are reinforced by failures to trigger-decode the narrative material that leave deep unconsciously experienced death issues uninterpreted. The resultant obliterating defences are thereby passed down from one generation of analysts and therapists to another—in both word and deed.

d. As for understanding and interpreting the conscious and deep unconscious meanings of death-related experiences, this work is confined to material from the superficial unconscious subsystem of the conscious system and possible early childhood connections, and it fails entirely to address deep unconscious expressions and their meanings.

e. Therapists attracted to these therapists and theories may be seen, in general, as wishing to deal fully with death anxiety, but as ending up with compromised efforts, much of them more intellectualized than narrative-based.

3. *Maximally open*

These are treatment modalities that (1) fully appreciate the role of frame-related interventions as related to efforts to adapt to death anxieties; (2) understand the need for secured frames and comprehend the existential anxieties they engender; (3) appreciate the traumatic, death-related character of frame modifications; (4) maximize patients' opportunities to communicate encoded narrative material, including emergent disguised images and stories that pertain unconsciously to death-related issues; and (5) make full use of trigger-decoding the disguised images evoked by death-connected triggering events in order to interpret validly a patient's unconscious death-related conflicts and defences.

a. To my knowledge, only the communicative approach can be placed into this category of treatment modalities. The standard form of communicative psychotherapy allows for this kind of work, and the empowered form greatly enhances it.

b. In order for therapists to conduct a soundly managed and well-interpreted secured-frame therapy, they must resolve aspects of their own death anxieties and conflicts and diminish their natural use of denial-based, communicatively obliterating defences.

c. Therapists drawn to the communicative approach seem to wish to deal most adaptively to death-related issues. However, in the real world of psychotherapy, many communicative therapists prove to be unable to hold frames secured and to offer sound, validated trigger-decoded interpretations when death-related triggers are at issue. This finding testifies to the great difficulties we, as therapists and humans, have in dealing with death anxieties and in changing our naturally maladaptive ways of coping with them—even when we are consciously motivated to do so.

* * *

With this in mind, let us turn now to the major means through which therapists defend themselves in psychotherapy against death anxiety and related problems.

CHAPTER FIFTEEN

How therapists defend against death anxiety

In the course of exploring therapists' attraction to the various modes of therapy, I have alluded to a variety of ways in which therapists defend themselves against death anxiety. Most of these efforts are maladaptive and exert a negative influence on their patients and their symptoms and coping efforts. While both patients and therapists defend themselves mightily against death-related issues, the specific forms through which these defences are effected very much depends, as noted earlier, on their respective role requirements and the constraints placed on them by the ground rules of therapy. This context offers a framework for exploring the favoured ways in which therapists defend themselves against death anxieties.

There is a critical distinction to be made between patients and therapists. The patient can be expected to make use of maladaptive defences against death anxiety, even when they are dysfunctional; their expression, interpretation, and resolution are an essential part of the therapeutic work. On the other hand, because these same defences severely interfere with a therapist's work—the offer of a sound process of cure through their ability to carry out the necessary frame-securing and trigger-decoded interventions—therapists are expected to have resolved or controlled their needs for these costly overprotective mechanisms.

At present, rather than pursuing this goal, therapists tend to accept the rationalized justifications that have led to the institutionalization of these defences in most forms of therapy, including psychoanalysis. Incorporation of this defensiveness into the fabric of various therapeutic techniques creates problems for dealing with patients' death anxieties, as well as difficulties in convincing therapists that they need to change so that they can position themselves to recognize expressions of death anxiety better and to deal with them therapeutically.

Therapists' main defences against death anxiety and death-related conflicts operate on three levels—communicative, psychological, and action/behavioural. While they are psychodynamically determined, they also arise fatefully from the architecture of the emotion-processing mind. Were the design other than it is, therapists would naturally be inclined to conduct psychotherapy in ways that would not so intensely reflect these unconsciously created and usually unrecognized defensive manoeuvres. Listing these defences also will make clear the differences in the specific form of defence against death anxiety adopted by patients and therapists. Let us look at each of these basic categories.

1. *Communicative defences*

Therapist's most commonly used communicative defences include the following:

a. Interfering with patients' narrative communications by means of a wide range of active interventions—for example, asking questions, confronting, advising, and so on. Unconsciously, these efforts are designed to eliminate or minimize death-related derivative or encoded expressions, and they convey a message to the patient to avoid this type of communication lest the therapist find it intolerable.

   When death-related issues have been activated, the use of these interventions tends to increase. Their application in any form unconsciously conveys the therapist's intolerance for unconscious meanings in this area, including the patient's unconscious perceptions of the therapist's own directly or indirectly expressed vulnerabilities in this regard.

b. Failing to understand properly a patient's encoded messages—being derivative-deaf (Langs, 1992). Through this defence, when a patient conveys encoded narratives, the therapist defends himself or herself by focusing on the surface meanings and implications of the patient's communications and thereby obliterates the encoded meanings of the material.

c. Failing to identify the key adaptation-evoking, death-related triggering events that are activating the patient's encoded imagery. This is especially true of death-connected events related to the therapist himself or herself and of defensive interventions designed unconsciously to defend against death anxiety, such as frame modifications—especially frame-altering self-revelations about personal ills.

   i. Therapists are disturbed by the devastating images of themselves that a patient states directly, but they are even more disturbed by the terrible and valid perceptions of themselves in light of their interventions that are encoded in a patient's narrative material. These incisive unconscious perceptions, which are personally selected by the patient, often reflect readings of the therapist's death anxieties and the defences against these anxieties. Unconsciously, they activate a host of self-protective, erroneous interventions by the therapist.

   ii. While death-related triggers that occur outside therapy are often addressed by these therapists, this is done in terms of manifest responses and their implications, and the encoded, deep unconscious meanings related to triggers within the therapy are overlooked.

d. Intervening in any manner except through valid trigger-decoded interpretations. In principle, all efforts that depart from the standard adaptation-oriented communicative approach inherently discourage a patient's inclination to narrate and generate encoded communications. These efforts also avoid the deep unconscious meanings of whatever the patient does communicate, especially as evoked by death-related triggers.

All in all, then, therapists' communicative defences against death anxiety are expressed through a variety of efforts to discourage the communication of encoded narratives from patients and through failures to appreciate their unconscious meanings when they are nevertheless expressed. While patients tend to defend themselves by not conveying encoded themes or their triggers, therapists tend to defend themselves by interfering with the patient's natural tendencies ultimately to communicate encoded meanings in their material. Often the result is a strong unconscious misalliance between patient and therapist that results in the destruction of meaningful unconscious communication as it pertains to death-related issues. Given the unresolved death anxieties of their mentors and themselves, and the support they obtain from their theoretical leanings and peers, therapists experience little or no conscious motivation to change this situation.

There are, however, certain real consequences to these non-validated, errant ways, and an unappreciated *unconscious motive* that exists in all therapists, that can move them to rectify these mistaken defensive techniques. It lies with the finding that therapists *unconsciously monitor* their therapeutic ministrations as they unconsciously affect their patients. The deep unconscious systems of psychotherapists are able unconsciously to perceive and trigger-decode patients' responses to their intervention in ways that are more compelling than anything that the conscious system can carry out. This unconscious monitoring is a continuous process, and it deeply and unknowingly affects a therapist's work and daily life.

The damaging consequences of interventions unconsciously fashioned to defend against a therapist's death anxieties, while usually not perceived consciously, are picked up in the therapist's own deep unconscious system and shunted to the guilt-containing part of the deep unconscious fear–guilt subsystem. In consequence of the *unconscious guilt*, the therapist is likely to become self-punitive and self-harmful in his or her therapeutic endeavours and daily life.

For example, a male therapist suffering from undue death anxiety may modify a ground rule of therapy—for example, by reducing his fee. The patient involved then steals money from the cash box at his office. The link to the fee reduction, which is a way of allowing the patient to deprive the therapist of income inappropriately, goes unnoticed consciously by either patient or therapist. But unconsciously the therapist recognizes the connection, feels guilty, and will respond accordingly with the patient, with other patients, and in his daily life. Not infrequently, the result is a provocative, self-harmful act by the therapist, such as being dishonest with money himself—for example, by cheating on his income tax in a way that is likely to be discovered.

If the sources of this unconscious guilt and these self-defeating behaviours are identified consciously and the erroneous techniques rectified, the therapist will do much better personally and with his or her patients. *Left unacknowledged and unresolved, unconscious guilt over failing their patients in an attempt to avoid dealing with death issues is a major cause of suffering by therapists for their very human but costly defences against death anxiety.*

2. *Psychological defences*

Therapists tend to favour particular forms of psychological defences against death anxiety. These include denial mechanisms through which death-related material is ignored, and repression through which this kind of material is not recollected in sessions as needed. Secondary defences are invoked to support these basic mechanisms, such as intellectualization, isolation, and reaction formation. In part, the overemphasis in psychoanalysis on intellectualized interventions and the stress on sexual conflicts, self-regulation, and object relations to the neglect of unconscious interaction, violence, and death are common means used to deny the greater threat to emotional equilibrium posed by death-related traumas and anxieties.

3. *Action/behavioural defences*

While all of the defences against death anxiety invoked by therapists involve a measure of activity on his or her part, the main denial-supporting, action form of defence vis-à-vis death issues is, as we have seen, the invocation of frame modifications in a psychotherapy experience. At times, these departures from the ideal frame are monumentally denial-based and damaging—as seen in any type of seductive overture by a therapist towards a patient.

These interventions function unconsciously to discharge and momentarily alleviate activated death anxieties, however maladaptively. They also discourage encoded communication from patients and enable therapists to avoid their patients' and their own secured-frame existential death anxieties. As a result, however, neither party to therapy has an opportunity to work over and better adapt to his or her fundamental death-related conflicts and anxieties—a necessary feature of any successful, deep form of therapy.

In general, the use of interventions that serve as maladaptive defences against death anxiety tend to be sanctioned in psychotherapy practices throughout the world today. We need at long last to recognize the unconscious defensiveness reflected in the many interventions that express these defences in the daily work of therapists. And we must also deal with the larger problem of diminishing their use and shifting to more adaptive and effective modes of treatment. Psychotherapists will need to carry out a great deal of personal self-searching and self-processing to achieve any significant changes in these troublesome areas.

DEATH ISSUES AND THE PSYCHOTHERAPIST

To conclude this chapter, let us look now at the kinds of problems that death and death-related issues may create for the psychotherapist. There are, of course, countless ways that death may become an adaptive issue for a therapist and greatly influence his or her therapeutic work—usually by creating pressures to modify frames and avoid encoded derivatives and their death-related triggers.

The following appear to be the basis for most of a therapist's immediate death-related problems:

1. A serious illness, injury, or death that befalls a member of the therapist's family or someone close to the therapist such as a colleague, friend, his or her own therapist, or one or more of his or her patients.
2. Serious illness or injury suffered by the therapist himself or herself, including occasions when the therapist is dying.
3. Reaching one's senior years. The ageing psychotherapist will experience significant, active, existential death anxieties and will tend to be especially vulnerable to predatory forms of death-related traumas such as injury and illness.

Two broad problems in technique arise from these death-related issues: (1) the need to cancel sessions suddenly because of a therapist's illness or severe injury, or an illness, injury, or death of one of his or her family members; (2) the handling of visible signs of illness or injury in the therapist.

DEATH-RELATED CANCELLATIONS OF SESSIONS

The ideal secured-frame approach to cancelling a session without advance notice is simply to miss the session and allow patients with appointments to come to the session, only to find the door locked and the therapist absent. A telephone call to the patient is frame-modifying in that it creates contact between patient and therapist outside the office and at a time other than the patient's session. It also entails a frame-breaking self-revelation and risks leaving a recorded message or making contact with a third party who happens to answer the patient's telephone. If the therapist elects to leave a message with that person, the deviation is compounded by involving a third party in the patient's therapy.

Therapists have difficulty with this approach because they tend to use social rather than therapy-related criteria for their decisions and behaviours. They also experience conscious concerns about disturbing and angering the patient with an unexplained absence and unnecessarily inconveniencing the patient who is allowed to come to a session that the therapist knows he or she will miss. However, these concerns, while realistic, are also unconsciously used to justify frame modifications that the therapist unconsciously uses to maladaptively reduce his or her own aroused death anxieties—death-denying fusion is a prominent psychological feature of these frame breaks.

The possibility of an unannounced extended absence from the office renders frame-breaking telephone calls to patients a practical necessity. If a date of return is clearly established, it should be announced to the patient when the call is made. If not, the patient should be told that the therapist will call back when he or she is ready and able to resume sessions.

In principle, the goal is to reveal as little as possible, to maintain a professional approach despite universal tendencies to cope with death anxiety by modifying the frame through personal self-revelations, and to keep the frame modifications to a minimum.

In calling the patient, the therapist should make the conversation as brief as possible, simply indicating that he or she is cancelling the session. No reason should be given—the emergency nature of the cancellation is implied by the call. No message should be left with a third party, and the therapist's home or hospital telephone number should not be given to the patient or to anyone with whom the patient has contact. Although intentionally and consciously considerate, it must be understood that the call is a frame modification and will be experienced as such unconsciously by the patient—with all of the attendant negative deep unconscious perceptions the frame break evokes.

Whichever way the therapist decides to manage the cancellation, the absence from one or more sessions and the presence or absence of a telephone call must be taken as prime triggering events for the sessions that follow. The patient's narrative material should be linked to the various triggers and interpreted, but in addition the frame should be rectified if called for. For example, an *unnecessary* telephone call will be encoded as inappropriate in the patient's material, and the therapist must use the patient's themes to promise not to call without good cause in future.

In these situations, if the patient does not allude to the trigger—a surprisingly frequent occurrence—the therapist technically may introduce it because it is an event that happened after the last session had been held. Derivatives that enable the therapist to use the patient's encoded images as a basis for doing so are always available.

The therapist who is unable to return to work because of a major disability or because he or she is dying has several additional problems to deal with. If able to come to the office to see patients, he or she should, of course, announce the impending departure directly to the patient and allow as many sessions as possible for the working-over of this highly traumatic death-related triggering event.

If the termination must be carried out by telephone, the call should be made by the therapist personally if at all possible. Telephone sessions modify the frame and are inadvisable, but some brief working-over of this rather drastic loss on the telephone may be helpful if the therapist is capable of doing it. If the situation requires a third party to make these calls, *another therapist should make them.* Having a family member make the calls compounds the deviation and burdens the caller and the patient severely, although it may be used as a last resort *and without that person identifying himself or herself*—an ideal that is difficult to adhere to.

As for the critical question of the patient's need for further therapy, the secured-frame intervention is to allow the patient to find his or her own way back into therapy. However, therapists who are convinced that a particular approach to treatment is especially valuable—as is the case with communicative psychotherapists—may refer patients to colleagues competent in these clinical methods.

THE EVIDENTLY ILL THERAPIST

Therapists who are suffering or recovering from an obvious or serious injury or illness should expect their patients to have strong unconscious responses to the trigger and a varying, often defensive conscious response as well. Many patients consciously fail to refer to an evident injury in a therapist, although the encoded narrative derivatives almost always do so. They are therefore available for a playback to the patient—the description of the patient's themes organized as clues to the unmentioned trigger (Langs, 1992)—and will often lead the patient to consciously acknowledge the trigger, on which basis his or her unconscious responses can then be interpreted. These are difficult moments for both patient and therapist, but the therapeutic work must be concentrated on the issues they raise unconsciously—and consciously as well.

THE AGEING PSYCHOTHERAPIST

With regard to the ageing psychotherapist, we may turn to an observation made by Freud (1926d [1925]) regarding the evolution of the primary anxieties in humans—a sequence he defined without including death anxiety. Freud postulated a series of primary sources of anxiety—in our terms, adaptive issues—that begin with the fear of the loss of the mother's love, and move to the loss of faeces, loss of the penis (castration anxiety), and, finally, the intrapsychic dread of the loss of the love of one's own superego.

Clearly, the loss of other loved ones and, especially, the fear of losing one's own life, are needed to complete this list of universal adaptive issues and sources of anxiety. This includes the existential forms of death anxiety which tend to intensify as the psychotherapist grows older. He or she must therefore maintain a careful eye towards the effects of these mounting anxieties. Specific death-related incidents will further aggravate these problems; they are triggering events that are especially likely to mobilize unconsciously a variety of adaptive but mostly maladaptive defences. The continual working over and working through of these anxieties, much of it through personal self-processing, should be a prime activity of the elderly therapist (Langs, 1993).

In time, these pursuits will culminate in a career-ending illness or injury or in the decision to terminate one's practice. In the latter case, several months should be allowed between the announcement of these plans—a form of *forced termination*—and its actualization, during which this anticipated, death-related triggering event must be used as a prime organizer of the patient's conscious and unconscious adaptive responses.

SUMMING UP

All in all, a psychotherapist's career begins with a significant death-related history and a set of adaptive and defensive preferences. As the career progresses, much is added to this history. Then, in the senior years—many therapists work well into their eighties and some into their nineties—death casts a long and ever-present shadow over their lives and work as therapists. Death is never far from the life and mind of the elderly psychotherapist and requires constant vigilance lest the effects of death anxiety lead to significant maladaptive actions with patients and in the everyday life of the senior therapist.

In this connection is well to stress the importance of personal self-processing for the psychotherapist, especially when a death-related event occurs within his or her practice or personal life. If a therapist fails to keep a deeply understanding eye on death, it will derail his or her work with patients and create vicious circles of unresolved death anxieties—defensive obliterations—technical errors—acting out with patients (including sexually)—unconscious guilt—further anxieties and error—further guilt—and so on. Extricating oneself from these downward spirals is difficult. As problematic and inescapable as it may be, death must be made less rather than more of a problem than it need be. The ageing therapist can learn and grow from the processing of death-related traumas and experiences that activate existential death anxieties.

Finally, we may wonder whether ageing therapists with their extremes of death anxieties and death-related traumas can function insightfully and within secured frames with their patients. There may well be a limit to what a therapist can tolerate with respect to death-connected traumatic triggers, beyond which the impulse to deny and obliterate and to break frames becomes unmanageable. Having the wisdom to know when one can no longer be an effective psychotherapist and having the strength to retire from practice when called for are virtues difficult to come by. A therapist is advised to engage in intense self-processing before conceding to these anxieties, but if all else fails, finding another profession may be best for death-sensitive therapists and their patients.

CHAPTER SIXTEEN

Death anxiety and problems of technique

Throughout this book, I have touched on problems of psychotherapy technique as they are affected by death-related issues. In this final chapter, I explore some selected but important issues of this kind and discuss their technical management.

ILLNESS, INJURY, AND DEATH DURING PSYCHOTHERAPY

Let us begin this final overview by reviewing and integrating the principles of technique that apply to the management of interludes during which illness, injury, and death take place in the life of either the patient or the therapist.

Death-related traumas for the patient

Inevitably, a therapist will be deeply affected by his or her patient's death-related experiences. These triggering events are processed by the therapist both personally and with the patient, in keeping with the therapist's death-related history, adaptive resources, and maladaptive defences.

Death anxieties evoke psychological, communicative, and action defences in both patient and therapist. The therapist should therefore be mindful of their likely activation and should interpret the patient's defences while endeavouring to keep his or her own defensiveness to a minimum; he or she also should avoid sanctioning or supporting the patient's maladaptive responses.

Special wariness should be afforded to the emergence of behavioural defences in the form of frame modifications—engaging in frame breaks at such times reduces the patient's expression of encoded narrative material and the insightful processing of his or her deep unconscious experience of the death-related trigger event. In addition, the loss of the secured therapy frame harms the patient psychologically at a critical moment through the loss of the therapist's holding qualities and the negative introject that the patient experiences. In addition, the invocation of a frame alteration reinforces maladaptive modes of coping with death anxiety.

With exceedingly traumatic death-related events, the patient will almost always intensify his or her communicative defensiveness and psychological defences against death anxiety to the point where any of the following may occur: an absence of trigger-decodable narratives; the communication of powerful narratives without the availability of the active triggers to which they need to be linked; an intensification of frame-altering behaviours; somatization; sexual acting out; and flight from a secured-frame-inclined therapist and therapy. Tolerant holding of the patient by the therapist until the necessary material is available for interpreting and frame managing is essential at such times.

In interpreting the patient's material during these interludes, it is critical to adhere to the principle that the patient's deep unconscious system is focused on the here and now of the therapy and especially on the therapist's current management of the ground rules. Thus, all deep interpretations must begin with triggers from within the therapy and the patient's unconscious perceptions of the therapist's efforts and only when relevant fan out from there into the external life situation of the patient.

In principle, then, therapists should refrain from offering direct comments and explanations of patients' reactions to death-connected events outside the therapy. Allusions to manifest contents discourage encoded communication and are seen unconsciously by patients as efforts by therapists to avoid the deeper meanings of these events—especially their encoded connections to frame-related triggering events within the therapy.

In these situations, the unconscious experience and meanings of the therapist's frame-management efforts will link unconsciously to the patient's working-over of the outside death experience. The therapist's actions will be viewed by the patient through the lens created by the recent trauma, and, in addition, personal genetic experiences connected to the triggers within therapy and the trauma outside treatment will also emerge—and be available for interpretation. The deep unconscious system operates in a particular way, and interpretations must be structured accordingly.

Finally, it is all too human for therapists, given their own unmastered death anxieties, to wish to become openly compassionate, non-interpretative, and frame-altering when patients are suffering from acute death-related traumas. It takes considerable strength to behave and intervene in the best interests of the patient's deep emotional needs and to refrain from such comments and actions. Sustaining a frame-securing and trigger-decoding/interpretative stance is, however, optimally therapeutic and deeply appreciated by the patient, who will benefit accordingly.

The dying patient

There are a number of special problems of technique that arise in connection with the dying patient, whether death is impending when the patient enters therapy or arises during the course of treatment. The key problem for the insight-oriented therapist is the central dilemma that he or she must face: on the one hand, the patient will encode his or her unconscious need for secured frames and deep unconscious trigger-decoded insight as a way of adapting to the prospect of dying. But, on the other hand, both the secured-frame and decoded death-related images may be devastatingly disturbing and unbearable for the patient—and often for the therapist as well.

This is a no-win/must-win situation for both patient and therapist. If the therapist holds the frame and trigger-decodes, he or she is of unique value to, and inherently supportive of, the patient at this time of crisis—deep insight is matchless for enabling patients to negotiate these troubled times. On the other hand, these interventions are also stressful for the patient, who may find them overwhelming and flee the therapy.

The problem is compounded in that the therapist who knowingly modifies the ground rules of therapy and works with surface meanings and ignores deep encoded meaning, is unconsciously experienced as terrified of death. The patient will then be inclined to terminate treatment because he or she cannot find the needed holding and insight. Either way, the risk of premature termination is high.

The careful exercise of clinical judgement is called for in these situations. Both patient and therapist are inching along a tight wire that calls for staying centred and maintaining their balance, leaning neither too far towards deviation and obliteration of unconscious meaning, nor too far towards insisting on a totally secured frame and every possible measure of deep insight. Nevertheless, major deviations, such as a therapist's personal self-revelations, social contacts between patient and therapist, and the therapist's involvement with third parties are best avoided. In contrast, minor deviations, like an extra session in response to a crisis request, may well prove to be therapeutic, even though it will be perceived unconsciously as seductive, infantalizing, and an indication of the therapist's own unresolved death anxieties. The interpretation of the unconscious experience of these deviations is an essential follow-up effort.

When a therapist does modify the frame with a dying patient, maladaptive and harmful consequences are very likely to occur. Deviations create the need, longing, and search for further deviations. The human mind is configured in such a way that even a single deviation creates a hunger for more deviations, and frame-breaking may become a maladaptive way of life for the patient within the therapy and outside it. As a result, the therapy may founder—either because the additional deviations requested by the patient interfere with the therapeutic process or because the patient will interrupt treatment if he or she does not obtain further frame-modifying concessions from the therapist.

As the situation spins out of control because of the excessive demand for frame modifications, the therapist will find it necessary at some juncture to hold or secure the frame. At this critical point in the therapy, the therapist should make certain to decode the patient's narrative material in light of the fresh frame-securing triggers. This is perhaps the only means through which the treatment can be stabilized and the patient afforded further help.

Death-related traumas for the therapist

In the course of a long and hopefully rewarding and successful career, sooner or later a psychotherapist will experience any number of death-related traumas. These include personal illness and injury or becoming fatally ill, as well as the illness, injury, or death of one or more patients or family members, friends, and other figures of importance in the therapist's life. All of these triggering events involve moments of activated death-related conflict and anxiety. They are especially trying times for the psychotherapist.

The key issues for technique have already been adumbrated. The impact of a death-related event on the psychotherapist generally evokes strong unconscious needs for defence-minded frame breaks and interpretative errors, some of them inadvertent and others deliberately utilized but erroneously rationalized. The unconsciously driven urge to modify ground rules is enormous at such times, and even with extreme vigilance *lapses are almost inevitable*. When they do occur, the therapist should become aware of them as quickly as possible, rectify the frame break to the greatest extent feasible—and trigger-decode the patient's narrative material accordingly. To break the frame is human, to re-secure it is a unique therapeutic gift to the patient.

In practical terms, this means that a therapist should not share the ill state of his or her health with patients, nor should a therapist reveal the existence of an illness in someone close. If the patient learns of such a situation from a third party, the therapist should neither affirm nor deny the information, but should treat it as a third-party frame-deviant self-revealing triggering event that the patient accepts as fact (and for which the therapist must bear ultimate responsibility). The exploration and interpretation of an unconscious experience of this type must proceed according to the patient's material, although false information about a therapist tends to fade away with time.

There is, however, a major technical problem in these instances—namely, that patients show a truly remarkable inclination to repress and deny these troublesome third-party death-related triggering events. Their own need for denial and obliterating communicative defences, especially with respect to the unconscious perceptions of their therapists, creates clinical interludes in which the narrative themes tend to be replete with relevant encoded allusions, and yet the therapist's playback of these themes fails to enable the patient to recall the powerfully repressed or denied traumatic trigger.

In all such instances, the therapist must refrain from introducing the missing triggering event. This intervention would be experienced as an assault on the patient's much-needed psychological and communicative defences, and it would so isolate the death-related trauma in the conscious system of the patient that the exploration of deep unconscious responses would prove unfeasible. In general, the premature conscious articulation of a repressed triggering event deprives the incident of its psychodynamic power and interferes with the meaningful working-through of the relevant deep unconscious aspects of the experience.

In response to this kind of premature intervention, the patient's unconscious focus will shift to working over the therapist's death anxieties and need to break the frame with his or her self-revelation, and the illness issue would become a secondary trigger. The therapy becomes centred on the therapist's dysfunctions rather than those of the patient, who would unconsciously adopt the role of therapist to the therapist—a harmful turn of events for all concerned.

When the trigger is the death of, or serious illness in, someone close to the therapist, both unconscious death anxiety and guilt are activated. Together they provoke errors in intervening and frame breaks, including sexual acting out within and outside therapy, that are both defensive and self-punitive. The therapist should be alert lest serious damage be done to his or her clinical practice at these times of heightened unconscious guilt. Often a vicious circle develops—the more destructive the therapist becomes, the greater the guilt, which in turn leads to more destructiveness to self, patients, and others. Self-processing is essential at these times; it is probably the only means through which these unfortunate needs and tendencies can be adaptively and insightfully brought under control and resolved.

WHEN THEMES OF DEATH APPEAR IN THE PATIENT'S MATERIAL

In general, a therapist is aware of a patient's death issues as well as his or her own. But there are many sessions in which the theme of death appears in a patient's narrative material and the activating triggering event is either unclear or unknown to both parties to the therapy. I therefore will conclude this study of death and psychotherapy with this question: What are the triggering events that tend to evoke death-connected themes in a patient's encoded images? That is, when death themes appear in a patient's material, what kinds of known and repressed triggers should the therapist be searching for?

To answer these questions, I will begin with the surface and move to the depths. The following triggers are characteristically and universally linked to death issues and images:

1. *A consciously known death-related event.* Whenever an illness, injury, or death occurs in the life of a patient, including anything known about the therapist in this regard, the patient will allude to it directly or through encoded death-related themes.
    a. For events in the outside life of the patient, this allusion is a representation of a triggering event located outside the therapy—a so-called *external triggering event.* The patient will, in general, work over this type of trauma manifestly and consciously, with little encoded imagery. However—and this is a critical technical point—*despite the reality of the illness,*

injury, or death, these allusions almost always encode an additional unconscious adaptive response to a major triggering event within the therapy.

It is therefore crucial that the therapist not abandon the communicative way of listening and formulating when dealing with events of this kind. The search for an additional repressed trigger within the therapy must be a central pursuit at such times—carried out, of course, in keeping with the usual rules and techniques of therapy. Many repressed triggers have been missed because a therapist naively and erroneously, usually for reasons connected with his or her own death anxieties, treats a serious illness or death in the life of the patient as it stands manifestly and misses its encoded meanings.

b. If the consciously known death-related event involves the therapist, the patient may allude to it directly and initially respond with conscious thoughts and feelings. However, the therapist must be attentive to the subsequent encoded narratives told by the patient so as not to miss the representations of the patient's deep unconscious experience of that triggering event.

2. *Frame modifications by the therapist and, more rarely, by the patient.* I have offered abundant evidence that therapists' frame breaks are unconsciously experienced by their patients as seductive, assaultive, and murderously destructive. Virtually every frame break by a therapist will therefore evoke death-related imagery as an encoded reflection of these qualities of the intervention. The frequency with which such themes arise in psychotherapy attests to the prevalence of frame deviations in today's treatment settings.

Because patients will unconsciously monitor and process their own frame impingements, the same principles apply to their frame modifications as well. But regardless of who may have initiated a given frame alteration, it is primarily the responsibility of the therapist to re-secure the frame and interpret the relevant narrative material in order to turn the interlude into a healing event for the patient—and for the therapist as well.

3. *Frame-securing interventions.* As we have seen, secured-frame moments in therapy evoke bi-phasic responses in patients—positive imagery followed by death-related themes. These latter themes typically allude to enclosures, entrapment, and annihilation. They need to be interpreted in light of the frame-securing triggering event to which they are an adaptive response. This work enables the patient insightfully to reduce his or her existential death anxieties—a very salutary piece of therapeutic work.

When death themes appear in the material from the patient, the therapist should look to the frame—in all likelihood, a ground rule has been modified or secured.

A FINAL PERSPECTIVE

Death is one of the most compelling and anxiety-provoking parts of life. Its many affiliated expressions arise in the course of a treatment experience when a ground rule is modified and when violence of any kind is at issue, physically or psychologically—whether within the therapy or outside it. Paradoxically, death is also evoked when a therapy is stabilized, and holding the patient and establishing a caring environment have been achieved through a securing of its frame. Death is also with us without mercy whenever illness, injury, or death itself impacts on the patient or therapist. Death is indeed an ever-present shadow cast over the lives and therapeutic work of all patients and therapists. The therapist who can secure a therapy frame and trigger-decode death-related imagery has mastered much of the art, power, and healing potential of deeply insightful, frame-securing psychotherapy. I very much hope that this book has illuminated the path to that mastery and significantly contributed to its achievement by the reader.

REFERENCES

Arlow, J., & Brenner, C. (1964). *Psychoanalytic Concepts and the Structural Theory*. New York: International Universities Press.

Baldwin, J. (1896). A New Factor in Evolution. *American Naturalist, 30*: 441–451, 536–553.

Becker, E. (1973). *The Denial of Death*. New York: Free Press.

Bickerton, D. (1990). *Language and Species*. Chicago, IL: University of Chicago Press.

Bickerton, D. (1995). *Language and Human Behavior*. Seattle, WA: University of Washington Press.

Burnet, F. (1959). *The Clonal Selection Theory of Acquired Immunity*. Nashville, TN: Vanderbilt University Press.

Calvin, W. (1991). *The Ascent of Mind*. New York: Bantam.

Cannon, W. (1929). *Bodily Changes in Pain, Hunger, Fear, and Rage. Researches into the Function of Emotional Excitement*. New York: Harper & Row.

Cziko, G. (1995). *Without Miracles*. Cambridge, MA: MIT Press.

Dawkins, R. (1983). Universal Darwinism. In: D. S. Bendall (Ed.), *Evolution from Molecules to Man* (pp. 403–425). Cambridge: Cambridge University Press.

Dorpat, T. (1985). *Denial and Defence in the Therapeutic Situation*. New York: Aronson.

Edelman, G. (1987). *Neural Darwinism*. New York: Basic Books.

Edelman, G. (1992). *Bright Air, Brilliant Fire*. New York: Basic Books.

Freud, A. (1936). *The Ego and the Mechanisms of Defence*. New York: International Universities Press; London: Hogarth Press. [Reprinted London: Karnac Books, 1989.]

Freud, S. (1915d). Repression. *Standard Edition, Vol. 14* (pp. 141–158).

Freud, S. (1920a). Beyond the Pleasure Principle. *Standard Edition, Vol. 19* (pp. 3–64).

Freud, S. (1923b). *The Ego and the Id. Standard Edition, Vol. 19* (pp. 1–66).

Freud, S. (1926d [1925]). *Inhibitions, Symptoms and Anxiety. Standard Edition, Vol. 20* (pp. 77–178).

Gazzaniga, M. (1992). *Nature's Mind*. New York: Basic Books.

Giovacchini, P. L. (1991). The Creative Person as Maverick. *Journal of the American Academy of Psychoanalysis, 19*: 174–187.

Jerne, N. (1967). Antibodies and Learning: Selection versus Instruction. In: G. G. Quarton, T. Melnechuck, & F. O. Scmitt (eds.) *The Neurosciences: A Study Program, Vol. 1* (pp. 200–205). New York: Rockefeller University Press.

Langs, R. (1982). *Psychotherapy: A Basic Text*. New York: Aronson.

Langs, R. (1988). *A Primer of Psychotherapy*. Lake Worth, FL: Gardner Press.

Langs, R. (1992). *A Clinical Workbook for Psychotherapists*. London: Karnac Books.

Langs, R. (1993). *Empowered Psychotherapy*. London: Karnac Books.

Langs, R. (1995). *Clinical Practice and the Architecture of the Mind*. London: Karnac Books.

Langs, R. (1996). *The Evolution of the Emotion-processing Mind: With an Introduction to Mental Darwinism*. London: Karnac Books; Madison, CT: International Universities Press.

Lieberman, P. (1991). *Uniquely Human*. Cambridge, MA: Harvard University Press.

Margulis, L., & Sagan, D. (1995). *What Is Life?* New York: Simon & Schuster.

Plotkin, H. (1994). *Darwin Machines and the Nature of Knowledge*. Cambridge, MA: Harvard University Press.

Slavin, M., & Kriegman, D. (1992). *The Adaptive Design of the Mind*. New York: Guilford Press.

Weil, S. (1972). *Gravity and Grace* (trans. E. Crawford). London: Routledge, 1992.

INDEX